KAMALA DAS

The Great Indian Trend-setter

JAYDEEP SARANGI

AUTHORSPRESS
Publishers of Scholarly Books

Worldwide Circulation through Authorspress Global Network
First Published 2010
by
Authorspress
E-35/103, Jawahar Park
Laxmi Nagar, Delhi-110 092
e-mail: authorspress@yahoo.com

Kamala Das: The Great Indian Trend-setter
ISBN 978-81-7273-549-4

Printed in India at Tarun Offset, Delhi.

Editor's Note

"*J.S:* Like Nilangshu, may I ask you, is not this candid and frank portrayal of female body anti-woman?

Sarojini Sahoo: Anti-heterosexual ideas were developed in feminism under the banner of the anti-pornography movement. It is believed that sex always remains as the centre of a feminist explanation of women's oppression and these ideas lead the feminists to go far away from heterosexual relationships.

In around seventies, we found that most of the feminists either were lesbians or were unmarried because of their anti-heterosexual feelings. But later in eighties, the "Feminist Sex Wars" started a controversy among feminists whether by supporting anti sex ideas, feminists are going to support the tools of oppression of women used by patriarchal society or not.

I think there are two rights women lack. One is a financial right and another is a bodily right. For the right of a woman over her own body, sexual freedom is an essential component. Financial empowerment is not the only achievement. There must be right over own body for a female. "

(Sarojini Sahoo in Conversation with Jaydeep Sarangi, *Muse India*, Issue 28, Nov-Dec 2009)

****

Kamala Das (Madhavikutty in her early days and Suraiya now as she has converted to Islam) is an iconoclast who has asserted her identity on the firmament of Indian English poetry by her honest and candid poetical lines that breaks through the hypocritical veneer of man-woman relationships in Indian traditional society. She is an Indian English poet, short story writer, novelist, playwright, essayist, nonfiction writer, children's writer, and autobiographer. Her poetry is a serious break from the erstwhile female Indian poets like that of Toru Dutt and Sarojini Naidu, but a celebration of the universal experience of self, love-despair, anguish, failure and disgust against the traditional mode of gender manifestation apprehended through a feminine Indian awareness.

Kamala Das' poetic corpus illustrates and explores on the struggle for power and autonomy by the women poets. Her poems have a narrative of power—a creation of a self-affirming way of life for the female protagonist as an intelligent, self-aware, confident and integrated personality with the aptitude and ability to live life on her own terms. The central action her poetry revolves round an encounter between a seemingly irresponsible female protagonist and the sea. The combat between the woman and sea is presented in the poem in the form of a dialogue—argument and counter argument follow each other in a persuasive battle of verbose expressions:

> You were pleased
> With my body's response, it's weather, its usual shallow
> Convulsions.
> You dribbled spittle into my mouth, you embalmed
> My poor lust with your bitter –sweet
> Juices.......

(*The Old Play House and Other Poems*: 17)

Kamala Das is at her poetic best a poet of private (confessional) sensibility. Her consciousness is firmly yoked to the world around her, a world characterized by ecstasy and pain, love and despair. At 42, she published her autobiography, *My Story*, baring the secrets of her heart. Her poems are gestures that counter the luridness of the world. Kamala Das's first volume of poems *Summer in Calcutta* (1965) arises from the poet's agonized response to the external world about the traumatic experiences of her childhood and early married life. The next collection *The Descendants* (1967) not only explores the leading motifs like love, lust and disillusionment, but also shows a metaphysical concern with time, death and decay. *The Old Playhouse and Other Poems* (1973) continues the poet's concern with the deeper meaning of life, death, disease and decay. In her *Collected Poems* (1984) we hear Kamala Das with a more mature and talented poetic voice. Her poetry collection published under the title, *Only the Soul Knows How to Sing*

(1996) is a touching account of a traumatic frustration in love and marriage. Irony assumes a tinge of social criticism in the short poem 'The Fancy Dress Show,' as the poet exposes the great fancy dress show, that is, our civilization.

> Every virtue requires today
> A fancy dress; the cassock is
> The priest's main virtue, the clever
> Politician dons a saint's mean
> Apparel.

Kamala Das's postcolonial concern for linguistic identity shows her honest commitment as a postcolonial writer:

> "I am Indian, very brown, born in
> Malabar, I speak three languages, write in
> Two, dream in one."
>
> ('An Introduction': Kamala Das)

In 'An Introduction', Kamala Das goes on to narrate her growing up to womanliness. Her 'Self' comes to the surface line at the encroachment of her freedom of expression; her right to self-expression which is a prelude to her right to gender equality. 'An Introduction' is Kamala Das' self-assertive statement attacking so-called conventionalism. In her frank poetic lines in the poem she advocates the rights of women. Coupled with her exploration of women's basic needs is an attention to eroticism. For her poetics, restrained love seems to be no love at all; only a total immersion in love experienced in union of bodies can do justice to her experience. She becomes a feminist writer by making her women conscious. Her poetry shows a landmark in her female journey from victimisation to consciousness. The essence of her poems is struggle about her own 'Self'. As the self, female self, in her takes different sociological roles, the ultimate self in her cries out honestly which, in fact turns out to be a collective cry. It is a cry for constructing female space and identity: 'I too call myself I' ('An Introduction': Kamala Das)

In 1975, for first time, the known grammarian Robin Lakoff claimed that there is a typical female language, very different from that of men, marked by the use of certain linguistic features such as hedging devices, tag questions, intensifiers and qualifiers, so-called "trivial lexis," "empty" adjectives, and rising intonation on declaratives. Kamala Das is a brand for New Female language.

Kamala Das is the motivating energy and guiding star for most of the contemporary Female poets of India; it is irrespective of class, creed, geographical position and caste. The young North East poetess Amanda Tongper is a glaring example of Kamala Das' influence who is a pure wonder and a dynamite in the reading world!

'It is I'
- by Amanda Tongper
Lipstick stained summer goodbye
And it cried hypocritical rain.
It wasn't the kind of rain that makes the pebbles dance like one possessed
Or make the leaves supple ...
It was a strange matter-of- fact downpour
Like hugs and kisses to leaving relatives who sat on brains till it turned soft.
Yes, I sat on summer
and melted its precious gold into worthless tears.
So I deserved its meaningless goodbye.
But niceties do not matter when you are a solitary progressive ape.
It is I who decide whether summer is sunflower or a slumberous bitch
Or winter an unholy shrine for moth-eaten prayers...
It is I who decide whether night is only a day that died
Or day, a night white-washed.
It is I who decide whether you should be a pebble I piss on
or a souvenir I place in my living room.
It is I who decide to measure the worth of my life
by the number of times I had risen from my ashes
And not by the number of torches that burnt me.
It is I who decide to live.
How I am greeted at the end is as insignificant as
the celebrated summer breeze is to a fading tombstone
Or my tears to a phone.

(Published in *SBJES*)

I thank all the learned contributors who had submitted the articles long back. I must take it granted that the articles are original and first-hand; views expressed in articles are their own.

At last, I extend my indebtedness to those who have helped me all-along and made this very special book possible. Hats off to inspiring letters and e mails from my academic friends from different parts of India and abroad. The book is dedicated to my loving daughter, Titas who turns seven this month. I thank Sutapa for her creative engagement with me.

I have applause for the publisher and those who stand with me always.

Jaydeep Sarangi

Notes on Contributors

Bikram Kumar Mohapatra, Deptt. of English, Brahmabarada College, JAJPUR, Jajpur-755005, Orissa.

K. S. Anish Kumar, 5/1, Gobi & Abi Illam, Jambu nagar II cross Mannacahanallur, Tiruchirapalli-621005. Tamil Nadu.

K V Dominic, PG Department of English, Newman College, Thodupuzha East P. O., Idukki-685585, Kerala.

Masoumeh M. Moradi, Ph. D Student, Mumbai Universit

B/33, Sumeru Apts., S. V. P. Nagar, Near Mahada Tel. Exg. Versova, Andheri (West), Mumbai-400053; Email: reyhane_m1360@yahoo. com

Muktha Manoj Jacob, H.O.D. of English, Narsee Monjee College Of Commerce & Economics, Mumbai-400056.

Neeru Tandon, Reader, Department of English, V.S.S.D. College, Kanpur, U. P.

Prajna Paramita Panigrahi, Lecturer in English, DDCE, Utkal University, Vani Vihar, Bhubaneswar, Orissa: State.

Purnendu Chatterjee, Research Scholar in English, Ogg Road, Noapara-743133, West Bengal.

Sheeba V. Issac, Research Scholar, Dept. of English, St. Thomas College, Pala, Kottayam-686574, Kerala.

Sobha Diwakar, MIG 33, Govind Bhavan Colony, South Civil Lines, Near Sai Mandir, Jabalpur - 482001, MP.

Sutapa Chaudhuri, 'Ashavari', L-58, Bosepara, Kamdahari, Garia, Kolkata-84, West Bengal.

Contents

1

'The Sea is Garrulous Today': Reading "The Invitation" by Kamala Das

— *Sutapa Chaudhuri*

Ultimately,
I have come face to face with the sea.
...
All I want now
is to take a long walk
into the sea
and be there, resting,
completely uninvolved.
But,
rest is only a childish whim,
a minor hunger.
Greater hunger lurks
at the basement of the sea. ("Composition")

...For long I've waited for the right one
To come, the bright one, the right one to live
In the blue... ("The Invitation")

Kamala Das is one of the best-known contemporary Indian women writers. Her poems are known for their provocative yet unflinchingly honest explorations of the female self and sexuality, urban life, women's roles in traditional Indian society, issues of postcolonial identity, and the political and personal struggles of marginalised people. Her poems are accounts of deeply personal experiences. But more than the confessional element, it is the brutal frankness of her verse that is the hall mark of her oeuvre. Kamala Das communicates a powerful female sensibility in her poetry and breaks the taboo by writing about sexual frustration and desire in women. She speaks of fantasies, of the disappointments of love, of the suffocation and futility of lust, of the loneliness and neurosis that stalk women. As such, her poetry speaks not only of her personal distress, but also of her outrage against the social norms of a patriarchal society.

Das's poems work at least at two levels. On the one hand, they depict a personal, a very individual tragedy. On the other, these poems are an attack on a way of life characterised by patriarchal norms which oppress and restrict women, reducing them to neurotic and pathetic creatures. The poems are also, ultimately, about women's struggle and survival. Das's poetical stance focuses on personal empowerment and autonomy; it showcases the politics of the integrity of the female self in a male-dominated and sexually predatory world. It is, ultimately, the politics of the survival not of the fittest, but even of those who are unable to fit in, those who are unfits and misfits in our society. Scholars such as Devindra Kohli, Eunice de Souza, and Sunil Kumar have found powerful feminist images in her poetry, focusing on critiques of marriage, motherhood, women's relationships to their bodies and power over their sexuality, and the roles women are offered in traditional Indian society.

Across time and space, the woman writer, especially the woman poet, is engaged in an on going dialectic with the dominant cultural hegemonies to negotiate a space for the creative woman, where authentic female experiences can be articulated freely. The poem "The Invitation" by Kamala Das amplifies, illustrates, and carries on this struggle for power and autonomy by the women poets. This poem is a narrative of power—a creation of a self-affirming way of life for the female protagonist as an intelligent, self-aware, confident and integrated personality with the aptitude and ability to live life on her own terms.

Like many of Das's poems, "The Invitation" is not easy to read and demands a close study of the text wherein a complex pattern has been infused into the loose structure of the poem. Frustratingly inconsistent, self-indulgent, and equivocal, the poem begins abruptly with a conversational tone and colloquial speech rhythm. The central action in "The Invitation" revolves round an encounter between a seemingly irresponsible female protagonist and the sea. The sea invites, encourages, even allures the young woman to join it—to 'come in' to its all embracing, allengulfing waters, to merge herself voluntarily, and consequently, be submerged. The sea is envisaged here as a conniving entity that tries to seduce the unsuspecting woman by its debonair looks and smooth talking. By the very slippery suavity of its looks and alluring false speech, the sea takes on a Satanic tone of deception trying to lure the elemental female to her downfall; but, unlike the gullible Eve of the male myths, who falls a prey to male deceptions, the female protagonist in Das's poem resists the temptation to merge with nature and, thereby, retains her individual identity. The invitation to submerge the female self that the sea so ostensibly offers to the woman, may also be an allusion to suicide—the socalled 'only respectable way out'—the common solution that the society prescribes for the fallen woman in order to avert possible slander to the family name.

In this poem, the woman endures, even encourages, the initial stages of the sea's aggression, gets into a stimulating, tantalising argument/discussion with her aggressor while seemingly giving in to its allurements, yet chooses her own time to counter the aggression and emerges victorious. Her selfawareness, selfconfidence and self control prevent her from falling a prey to the death lures of the sea that signifies the ultimate dispossession of her self and total annihilation. The aggressive alluring sea masks its own duplicity by using enticing language; in an act of apparent kindness and consideration for the woman, the seemingly empathetic sea encourages and invites her to embrace its engulfing waters and thus be submerged.

The combat between the woman and sea is presented in the poem in the form of a dialogue/debate; argument and counter argument follow each other in a persuasive battle of words, where each of the opponents tries her/its best to outwit the other. The title of the poem raises some expectations in the readers through its multiple prior texts. 'Invitation' mostly signifies a kind of mutuality, the sense of belonging, a kind of communication, something positive, progressive, and lifeaffirming—a gesture signalling a happy social gathering or event that celebrates life and companionship. It shows a positive attitude towards life and self. But this very note of happy mutuality is abruptly curtailed by the bizarre image of a man's fist pounding inside the narrator's head. Pounding/hurting rhythmically, 'clenching, unclenching' like the surging, receding waves of the sea, holding and releasing pain alternately.

Significantly the gender of the 'I'—the first person narratorprotagonist of the poem — is withheld throughout the poem. Only through suggestive hints can we infer that the identity of the narrator of the poem is female. Notably, the focaliser in this poem is also the female protagonist herself. This is established by the first three lines. It is the voice of the female protagonist that we hear at the very outset of the poem and in between. It is also the very last voice that we hear, as if the narrative is framed by the voice of the narrator-focaliser. This technique gives the sense that it is basically the story of the female narrator in which the speeches of the sea are seen as intrusions. The sea is inviting, indeed imploring, her to commit suicide, and she has, presumably, all the reasons for it, yet she makes a positive lifeaffirming choice by firmly refusing to take the plunge. Rather, her resistance to a total merger with her mate gets gradually worn off by the sea's insistence on the negative choice. Instead of embracing suicide and annihilating herself forever, the female protagonist opts for mutuality that will finally prove to be creative and life generating.

The woman persona of many of Das's poems represents a split mutilated self tormented by both past and present, and resulting in a deep sense of crisis. Das's poems explore this duality that is best described as an opposition women feel between essential aspects of the self, between what is socially prescribed on the basis of gender and what is defined on the basis of the self, between what a woman feels she should be and what she feels she is. The persona in "The Invitation" too constantly pits herself against cultural expectations of 'Womanhood' — the self-crippling, selfdenying, self-distorting stereotypes who force themselves into the male sanctioned moulds. In the end, she redefines herself and liberates herself both as a woman and a creator, reclaiming her own identity.

In male writing, women have been equated with nature for centuries. They have been thought of as being an integral part of nature. But in the writings of women, significantly, nature and women are often shown as adversaries engaged in a deadly battle of power. This battle is based on nature's need to appropriate the female within its own hierarchical systems and the female need to resist it and retain her autonomy. In Kamala Das's poems, the sea is a predominant and recurrent image. It is related both to her moods of anguish and release. It sometimes becomes an extensive symbol, a thread that unifies her poetic experiences and images into one unified whole. An integral part of her elemental symbolism, the sea imagery serves the purpose of a retreat from the scorching world of the Sun. The sea-imagery occurs in many poems of hers, such as "The Descendants", "The Invitation", "Convicts", "The Sea Shore", "The Joss-Sticks at Cadell Road" and "The High Tide" to name a few. Her response to the concept of the 'sea', however, varies in her poems.

In "Advice to Fellow Swimmers", the sea functions as a refuge, a destination for safety that encourages the narrator to counsel her fellow swimmers to

> go swim in the sea,
> go swim in the great blue sea.

In "The Descendants" the sea becomes a kind of receptacle—the receptacle for human life. In "The Suicide" the sea image operates forcefully. "The Suicide" is a monologue addressed to the sea where the sea promises the perennial shelter of death. In this poem the sea is made an associate of 'the soul' discarding 'the body' away:

> I throw the bodies out,
> I cannot stand their smell.
> Only the souls may enter
> The vortex of the sea.
> Only the souls know how to sing
> At the vortex of the sea.

The 'sea' is the bedroom for her 'swimming.' As a child, she had swum into it; as an adult, she again wishes to swim into it and thereby quench her thirst for emotional contentment. She says:

> O sea, I am happy swimming
> Happy, happy, happy.....

She knows that 'water' is the prime mover of life, signifying the procreating power of the mother. It is easy for her to 'hold' it as a woman, but it is pretty difficult to 'hold' the love of her man. Her desire for fidelity in love has been shattered by him and she cries out in pain and dejection:

> Holding you is easy
> Clutching at moving water,
> I tell you, sea,
> This is easy.
> But to hold him for a half a day
> Was a difficult task.
> It required drinks
> To hold him down.

In a way, she herself is the holder of 'water' as she, too, is a mother yearning for peace, happiness and security. But her 'water' is not sufficient to intoxicate a man, and so he needs 'drinks' to make himself warm and jubilant. Towards the close of the poem, her identification with the sea is obvious—they are both 'generous' and 'sentimental', and that accounts for their being 'big flops':

> O sea
> You generous cow
> You and I are big flops
> We are too sentimental
> For our own
> Good.

The poem *"Composition"* depicts her childhood memory of the sea as 'the winds ceaseless whisper in a shell' which changes into the sound of 'the surf breaking on the shore.' The sea was within a walking distance from her Malabar house and provided her with rest and comfort and a life without 'involvement'. In "Composition", however, the sea also has the association with danger. In this poem, the hint of an encounter between the female narrator and the ruthless sea is prominent. The female narrator confesses the final outcome of her life:

> Ultimately,
> I have come face to face with the sea.

The very nearness of the sea with its "ceaseless whisper" of danger and the sound of angry "surf breaking on the shore" never proved to be a matter of consternation for the young narrator secure in a loving companionship. As a mature woman, she wishes to return to this sense of security and refuge that she enjoyed as a child and voluntarily desires to encounter the sea:

> All I want now
> is to take a long walk
> into the sea
> and be there, resting,
> completely uninvolved.

Her attraction for it, she clarifies later, is 'a childish whim,' a thing associated with her dreamy past:

> But,
> rest is only a childish whim,
> a minor hunger.
> But she is aware that
> Greater hunger lurks
> at the basement of the sea.

'Greater hungers' point not only to the elemental hungers of love and sex but also to selfannihilation. The matured female narrator now recognises the sea as one of the "devourers who constitute the world" whose aim is "to crumble, /to dissolve" and 'trap' the female self into "cages of involvement". This knowledge brings the awareness in the female narrator that even in dire conditions women must "retain in other things/the potent fragments/of one self" which will lead to "the ultimate discovery" that "we are immortal".

In "The High Tide" the sea is analogous to the rising passion within her:

> It's only the wind knocking at the door, the sea
> Is wild this morning, there is perhaps a high tide on...

In the poem "The Joss-Sticks at Cadell Road" that stresses the futility of the physical love, the sea becomes a receptacle of 'the poor men's bodies,' which burn like joss-sticks. In "Convicts", Das evokes the image of the post-sexual experience in the dark room through the sea:

> Darkness we grew as in silence
> We sang, each note rising out of
> Sea, out of wind, out of earth and
> Out of each sad night like an ache

In "The Invitation", the narrator's struggle with the sea continues. Here the female narrator, ostensibly, is suffering from a trivial, typically female ailment—"all the Sunday evening pains" of boredom and loneliness. She visits the sea in order to escape her suffering. She has often gone to the sea before as is suggested in another poem, "I have lived beautifully":

> I often walked with young man along the sea
> flaunting my unconventionality.

In another poem the female narrator says:

> When you leave, I drive my blue battered car Along the bluer
> sea.

But the sea had seemingly remained silent on those visits. Seeing her alone, lonely, and sensing her vulnerable mood, the sea suddenly becomes talkative: "The sea is garrulous today", observes the narrator, hinting that she is aware of some hidden, ulterior motive behind this change in the sea's behaviour. The sea slyly tries to persuade the lone protagonist to embrace its cool waters—to commit suicide so as to discard her isolated existence that can only offer the pain of alienation and loneliness. The sea invites the narrator very cordially like a loving friend to 'come in' to its cool, dark, deeps to ease her pain:

> The sea is garrulous today. Come in,
> Come in. What do you lose by dying, and
> Besides, your losses are my gains.

The female protagonist has nothing to lose by dying, argues the sea, as she is already dead emotionally/socially—she has been betrayed in her love by her lover—she has failed in sustaining a loving relationship; in other words, literally, she has failed to keep her 'man', the only socially sanctioned pivot/axis of her existence as a woman. Suicide, thus, should be a tempting option for her, as, according to the sea, she has nothing to live for. Suicide, notably, is also the socially acceptable way out for the betrayed and as such fallen woman. The female protagonist, however, ignores the solicitations of the enticing sea. She is keen on preserving her own identity, her autonomy. She is quite capable of living her own life in her own way. She does not need any advice; for, as she says, she does not care what the sea does: "slosh up, slide down, go your way", retorts the narrator and fervently wishes that the sea would be as indifferent to her as she is to it and let her be herself—let her "shrink or grow". She is clearly irritated by the sea's uncalled for intervention in her life for she prefers to live her own life according to her own rules. "I will go mine", she asserts emphatically:

> Oh Sea, let me shrink or grow, slosh up,
> Slide down, go your way.
> I will go mine.

Significantly, her life is a life of reminiscences. Her replies to the sea's arguments read like a monologue—a private reverie of her memories with her man, her lover who has betrayed her and left her alone. Yet her monologue about her lover and their lovemaking is interspersed with irritated interjections to the sea to leave her alone. These interjections function to establish a kind of dialogue and mutuality, a kind of communication between the woman and the sea. They also cut through her daydreams about her fond memories to uncover the reality beneath. They are her only links to sanity and the real world. She is living a life of memories and refuses to accept the reality of her situation. She still dreams about the moments of mutuality that she seemingly shared with her man. But slowly in her unconscious mind the image of the enticing sea and the treacherous lover merge, like "a fish coming up for air". "He came to me between/Long conferences". They merge because both of them offer her the same thing—betrayal and annihilation of herself.

> He came to me between
> Long conferences, a fish coming up
> For air, and was warm in my arms
> And inarticulate...

The image of the fish coming up for air is highly significant. 'Air' is needed for sustenance of life by the fish—an inhabitant of the sea—a creature wholly dependent on the sea for its life, and it is as slippery as the sloshing, sliding sea. The male lover, presumably a denizen of the sea, who has silently slipped away leaving the woman waiting vainly for his return, used to come to the woman for the renewal of his life sustaining force. He came to take a break from the monotony, the boredom, and the lethargy of his daily routine full of 'long conferences' and cold, calculative speeches. The word 'conferences' is also very significant here. Conferences are places for negotiations, for making deals, buying, selling and exchanging of opinion and material advice. This word highlights the multiple arrays of binary oppositions on which the poem is structured. For example, loneliness vs. companionship, mutuality vs. indifference, self vs. other, warm vs. cold, life vs. death, nature vs. humanity, personal vs. commercial, emotion vs. intellect, silence vs. speech, loss vs. gain, construction vs. destruction, and so on.

The lover is likened to a fish coming up for fresh air and diving deep when the need is over. The image of physical love and note of betrayal go together. She knows that 'the man is gone for good', and it would be foolish to wait for him - as the angry sea interjects. But the memory lingers on and the pangs of separation abides. Thus she recalls:

> On the bed with him, the boundaries of
> Paradise had shrunk to a mere
> Six by two and afterwards, when we walked
> Out together, they
> Widened to hold the unknowing city...

By trying to be her confidante and gain her confidence, the sea hides its true colours, its own intentions of betraying the unsuspecting woman but the word 'other' in "I want no other" shows that the woman is aware of the duplicitous nature of the sea. Both the 'inarticulate' lover and the 'garrulous' sea have the same intention—using the woman for their own gains. In return both of them offer her only momentary physical pleasures—one warm and the other cold but the goal of both is sleep—and the ultimate sinking into oblivion. Significantly the sea's arguments as well as the lover's gestures are focused on the woman's body

— "yourself lying on the funeral pyre", "stretch your limbs", "pillow your head", or "was warm in my arms", "our limbs inert, cells expanding/Into throbbing suns". The sea's relationship with the woman is also based on the opposition between self and the other, loss and gain—"your losses are my gains". For the woman, the relationship is much more distant and not at all economic—it is always in the impersonal third person. She calls the sea distinctively and repetitively by its generic name "sea" and never "you" but her relationship with her male lover is based on the relation of the self to her counterpart. It first starts with the tension of 'I', 'me'/'he', 'him' but before long it is 'we', 'our', telling of an established mutuality, till finally in the last line of the poem, the man is addressed directly by an endearment, "darling", and her own female self is described as 'one'—a neutral pronoun to denote that after voicing the biological woman's need for the biological man for "construction and destruction", the complete merger of the two binary selves becomes an actuality.

The invitation of the sea is alluring but the protagonist resists it; thus affirming her own individuality, her identity—her need is, not for a total merger, but to articulate her desires, and live up to her own potentials. The female protagonist in this poem denies and turns away from a negative, subordinate, submissive role—she refuses to get submerged, washed away, engulfed in the cold waters; her selfhood and identity obliterated for ever in the conventional codes and categories.

The sea in Das's poem promises to be a faithful, sympathetic, understanding and loyal companion who will help heal the hearts inflicted by the male world, through love, yet, in reality, it is itself a killer. The invitation is a death lure, and the waters, instead of proving embalming, will ultimately devour and destroy the woman. Instead of giving a shelter to the lost, homeless and socially outcast woman, it will take away surreptitiously the very land she is standing on—the 'cool secret' sands are as treacherous as quick sands and would engulf anyone who ventures to set foot on it. The promise is also sterile, the sea can only offer her death 'on a funeral pyre', not life, not creativity, for the salty waters themselves can bring only rot and wreckage. The sea tempts the female protagonist to embrace a negation of life—its promises, though alluring and magical, can have in reality, only negative associations and aspects for her. The dark waters of the sea symbolise death—it fails to hold any promise of a renewal or betterment or progression of life. The raging vortex of the black endless waters of the sea promise only annihilation. It offers a perennial shelter but of a negative kind—a home where instead of companionship and integration, she will face loneliness and disintegration; instead of affirmation, annihilation; instead of selfrealisation and mutuality, destruction and total obliteration. She would be in a position where 'even sinking would make no difference' ("Advice to fellow swimmers") and the only freedom she would have is 'the freedom to/ discompose' ("Composition").

Significantly one of the arguments given by the garrulous sea is that death by water is a more desirable and peaceful option for the young woman. The dark womb of the sea does not hold any promise of a renewal. It only promises the peace that comes from a complete negation of life.

> Bathe cool,
> Stretch your limbs on cool
> Secret sands, pillow your head on anemones,

The disintegration of the body in its waters is a gain to the sea, as it would prove, once and for all, its annihilating power, its ability to master the powers of the Almighty. According to the sea, it is also a gain to the invited one as it saves her the torture of being burnt on a funeral pyre. Tactfully hiding its true intentions, the sea offers a kind of metamorphosis for the female protagonist to embrace—a life of perfect peace inside the cool, blue waters. Yet, both the temptations, one by the sea and the other by her lover mean death to her—both of them offer her a complete negation of life, identity and selfhood. The outstretched lap of the sea offers her tired limbs 'cool secret sands' to relax and 'anemones' to pillow her head; the lover tempts her with tantalising memories of warm lovemaking 'on beds' all through sultry 'summer's afternoons' 'our limbs inert, cells expanding/Into throbbing suns':

> All through that Summer's afternoons we lay
> On beds, our limbs inert, cells expanding
> Into throbbing suns. The heat had
> Blotted our thoughts.....

The woman is haunted by both the cool, alluring invitations of the sea and the warm memories of her lover. She finally releases herself from the sea's tantalising promises by refusing to sink her identity as a woman and her individuality in the unknown and abysmal oceanic deeps. Her refusal to the sea's invitation makes her more intensely conscious of the precarious situation as she cannot escape the 'prying' eyes of the sea. Even the seemingly sympathetic fish, a creature of the sea, is in constant conspiracy with the prying sea in intruding her privacy. She sees through the enticing veneer of the sea to understand the destructive overwhelming force behind. Her refusal also brings to the light the real nature of the dark sea as a kind of hungry predator waiting patiently for centuries for the right prey to fall to its clutches and be a prisoner forever:

> For I've waited for the right one
> To come, the bright one, the right one to live
> In the blue.

The categorical "No"—the final rejection of the sea by the young woman — forces the raging sea, angry and frustrated, to retreat:

> The tides beat against the walls, they
> Beat in childish rage...

Her refusal takes away and ultimately denies the powers of the Almighty that the sea so fervently desires. The sea retreats in impotent rage, beating its waves in a futile effort to crumble the wall of resistance erected by the woman's refusal. It is her power to choose her way of life, which makes the female protagonist invincible.

From a life on the threshold, full of memories, the woman finally takes on a more challenging life—that of reality. She voices her needs and desires that she has been denying throughout her life and thus acknowledges herself as an integrated, individuated, self aware person. Her empowering decision to bond with her biological mate rather than with nature/sea, takes away all the barriers of loneliness and betrayal in her life and she becomes one with her lover. Thus her memories of assumed mutuality become a reality. The male lover, who, throughout the poem, has lived only in the memory of the female narrator and been presented as being absent in her life is now directly addressed, making him an active and realistic part of the narrative. She finally accepts death, a metaphor often used for the consummation of love, not in the depths of the cool embalming waters of the sea but the warm embrace of her human lover. She wipes out her bitter memory of being jilted in love and invokes the lover:

> Darling, forgive, how long can one resist?

The barriers, rifts that had separated them have all vanished; the two lovers have merged completely so that only love and oneness remain. The invitation of the sea to the woman to commit suicide, instead of being fatal, has turned out to be a boon, a blessing for the woman. It has incited the woman to acknowledge herself and voice her own needs. It has made her face reality, realise her dreams and empowered her to live life on her own terms. Because of the invitation to death, the female protagonist has made a life affirming choice by resisting it and realising her vocation in life—to achieve mutuality with her fellow human being and asserting her right to life. Instead of choosing destruction she ultimately embraces a creative path to life, thus denying the traditional choice of a woman forced to commit suicide to avoid defamation. She bests the sea so as to

> Fetter that ominous wail
> Let only silence move them
> Humming a slow
> And languid air.
> (*The Conflagration*: Kamala Das)

Works Cited

Bhatnagar, M.K. and Rajeswar, M.(Ed), *Indian Writings in English*, Atlantic Publishers and Distributors, New Delhi, 2002.

Deshpande, G.(Ed.), *An Anthology of Indo-English Poetry*, Hind Pocket Books Pvt. Ltd., Delhi.

Parthasarathy R.(Ed.), *Ten Twentieth-Century Indian Poets*, OUP, New Delhi, 1976.

Prasad, H.M. & Singh, C.P.(Ed.), *Indian Poetry in English,* Sterling Publishers Pvt. Ltd., New Delhi, 1985.

Rahman, A. *Expressive Form in the Poetry of Kamala Das,* New Delhi, Abhinav Publication, 1981.

Singh, K.D., *Feminism and Postfeminism: The Context of Modern Indian Women Poets Writing in English,* Sarup & Sons, New Delhi, 2004.

Sharma, R., *Split-Self and Self Assertion in The Poetry of Kamala Das,* http://www.goarticles.com/cgi-bin/showa.cgi?C=1003675

— *Emergence of Feminist Perspective in Recent Indian-English Woman, Poets,* http://thehoustonliteraryreview.com/Documents/Sharma_review_Emergence.pdf.

— Indian Feminist Perspective, *Muse India,* Issue 20, Jul-Aug 2008, http://www.museindia.com/showcurrent9.asp?id=997

Dwivedi, A.N., *Kamala Das and Her Poetry,* New Delhi, Doaba House, 1983.

Banerjee, L., "Modern English Poetry by Women: A Critical Survey in the Context of Feminism and Commonwealth Literature", *Journal of English Studies,* Vol-1, No-1 (Summer, 1995) Ranchi University, Ranchi.

2

A Feminist Reading of Kamala Das's Poetry

— K.V. Dominic

Kamala Das is beyond doubt the greatest woman poet in contemporary Indian English literature. A confessional poet, she displays feminist ethos in her poems.

Kamala Das, born in Kerala in 1934, is a bilingual writer. She writes in Malayalam, her mother tongue, under the pseudonym Madhavikkutty. She is the recipient of several prizes and awards: the P. E. N. Asian Poetry Prize, Kerala Sahitya Academy Award for fiction, Asian World Prize for literature, Kendra Sahitya Academy Award etc. She was short listed for the Nobel Prize along with Marguerite Yourcenar, Doris Lessing and Nadine Gordimer.

Her poetical collection includes: *Summer in Calcutta* (1965), *The Descendants* (1967), *The Old Playhouse and Other Poems* (1973), *Collected Poems I* (1984), *The Best of Kamala Das* (1991) and *Only the Soul Knows How to Sing* (1996).

Kamala Das's English poetry has been published in Europe in French, German, Swedish, and Serb-Croat translations. She "wrote chiefly of love, its betrayal, and the consequent anguish, and Indian readers . . . responded sympathetically to her guileless, guiltless frankness with regard to sexual matters. Ms. Das abandoned the certainties offered by an archaic, and somewhat sterile, aestheticism for an independence of mind and body at a time when Indian women poets were still expected to write about teenage girlie fantasies of eternal, bloodless, unrequited love" (*The Histrionics of Kamala Das*).

While reviewers of Das's early poetry praised its fierce originality, bold images, exploration of female sexuality, and intensely personal voice, they lamented that it lacked attention to structure and craftsmanship. Scholars such as Devindra Kohli, Eunice de Souza, and Sunil Kumar find powerful feminist imagery in Das's poetry, focusing on critiques of marriage, motherhood, women's relationship to their bodies and control of their sexuality, and the roles women are offered in traditional Indian society. Much criticism analyses Das as a "confessional" poet, writing in the tradition to Sylvia Plath, Anne Sexton and Denise Levertov. Some scholars, such as Vimala Rao, Iqbar Kaur, and Vrinda Naur, find Das's poetry, autobiography and essays frustratingly inconsistent, self-indulgent, and equivocal, although they, too, praise her compelling images and original voice. They suggest that Das is both overexposed and overrated. Other scholars, such as P. P. Raveendran, connect the emphasis on the self in Das's work to larger historical and cultural contexts and complicated, shifting postcolonial identities (*Das, Kamala*).

Kamala Das had an unhappy, dissatisfied life even from her childhood. She was a victim to patriarchal prejudices and discriminations as most women are. She converted to Islam in 1999 taking a new name, Kamala Surayya. It was an action, she said, she had been contemplating for many years. To quote her:

> Two plain reasons lured me to Islam. One is the Purdah. Second is the security that Islam provides to women. In fact, both these reasons are complementary. Purdah is the most wonderful dress for women in the world. And I have always loved to wear the Purdah. It gives women a sense of security. Only Islam gives protection to women. I have been lonely all through my life. At nights, I used to sleep by embracing a pillow. But I am no longer a loner. Islam is my company. Islam is the only religion in the world that gives love and protection to women. Therefore, I have converted. (*Kamala Das*)

The paradox of this conversion is that years later she confessed that it was a folly to convert from Hinduism to Islam. The reason is known only to her. It might be a reaction of the people's both her friends and foes—inhospitable and wounding response to her conversion. Dr. V. Alexander Raju is of the opinion that the conversion was an inevitable metamorphosis. To quote him, "In the poems of Kamala Das, we find a rare body and its feelings, and she seems incapable of thinking of eternal life as a bodiless existence. This peculiar stance may be the reason why she is drawn to Islamic religion with its different concept of life after life" (Raju 25). Frustrated by love and loneliness, she longed for an eternal life with her body and soul after her life on the earth. She loved her body as much as she loved her soul. Since her bodily desires could not be satiated by her life here she wants to achieve it by a life after death. As Hinduism could not promise her such a life, she converted to Islam. By conversion she reserved a life after life where she could attain the spiritual fulfilment in man-woman relationship which she missed, fortunately or unfortunately, in her earthly life.

Her conversion caused much ire and furore among Hindu fanatics and they started threatening her through letters and phone calls. Most dejected she bade goodbye to her ancestral house and native place, and sought refuge in her son's house in Mumbai. She is living there now fighting against old age problems.

Women's literature is different from feminist literature. Women's literature which results out of women's identity struggles creates new awareness in men and women whereas feminist literature expresses the shared experiences of women's oppression. "Feminist literature highlights and condemns the inequalities and injustices in the treatment of women—the disadvantages women have to bear on account of their gender" (Kumar 9). Its emphasis is on the ideology rather than on the literariness of the text. Feminism evolved as an opposition to patriarchy or the dominant sexist ideology.

It is customary for the much-centred aesthetic to consider artistic creation as an act analogous to biological creation. Thus an art work is the product of the interaction between the male artist and the external world which is regarded as feminine. A literary text in this view is the outcome of a generative act involving the phallic pen and the virgin blank page. A woman writer feels artistic creation as a form of violation, resulting in the destruction of the female body. In women's writing sexuality is identified with textuality. As a woman judges herself through her body, the female self is always identified with the female body in women's literature (Kumar 12-13).

A woman considers her role of mother more important than a wife. Wholly dependant on man in the world of his making, a woman craves to have a child for self-expression as a self-affirmation. In addition to sexual exploitation and betrayal the lack of love in a man-woman relationship is an improvised form of male oppression. Loveless relationships are unbearable for women. In the words of Prasantha Kumar:

> Kamala Das conceives of the male as beast wallowing in lust with a monstrous ego under which the women loses her identity. The strong desire for freedom, including the freedom to rebel, forms the central strain in many of her poems. She enumerates the male felonies in her poems and builds up a structure of protest and rebellion in her poetry. . . . Several poems of Das convey the tedium and monotony of sex within and outside marriage. . . . Their love is a disgusted lust, a poor substitute for real love. The life of Das's persona may be considered a tale of her experiments with love and the repeated failures of her experiments force her ego to be resentful and defiant. She looks upon each encounter as a substitute for the real experience of true love. (34-35).

Even as a child, Kamala Das experienced the bitterness of sexism. She was a victim of patriarchal prejudice. In her autobiographical book *My Book,* her "father was an autocrat" (91) and her mother "vague and indifferent" (20). Her parents considered her "a burden and responsibility and she was given in marriage to a relative when she was only a school girl" (82). Thus she was compelled to become a premature wife and mother. She complains about it in her poem "Of Calcutta":

> I was sent away, to protect a family's
> Honour, to save a few cowards, to defend some Abstraction,
> sent to another city to be
> A relative's wife.
>
> (*Collected Poems I,* 56-60)

In the same poem she presents the image of a doll to portray a woman's miserable condition: "Yet another nodding / Doll for his parlour, a walkie-talkie one to / Warm his bed at night" (*Collected Poems I,* 56-60).

The indifference of man to woman's miseries is depicted in her poem "The Stone Age." To quote from it:

> You turn me into a bird of stone,
> a granite dove,
> you build round me a shabby drawing room
> and strike my face absentmindedly while you read.
>
> (*The Best of Kamala Das,* 97-98)

When Kamala Das understood that love and matrimony are poles apart, she searched for a lover. "Though the love affair gives her excitement in the beginning it is accompanied by disillusionment. Her lover is incapable of giving her a blissful experience" (Raveendran 16). Thus her frustration is expressed through her poem "The Freak":

> . . . Can this man with
> Nimble finger-tips unleash
> Nothing more alive than the
> Skin's lazy hungers? . . .
>
> (*Only the Soul,* 59)

The woman's spirit of rebellion against male domination and ego is found in the poem "The Conflagration." As Dr. N. Sharda Iyer writes, "There is a degree to extricate front this 'Soul Killing' subjugation":

> Woman, is this happiness, this lying buried
> Beneath a man? It's time again to come alive.
> A world extend a Pot beyond his six foot frame.
>
> (qtd. in Iyer, 214)

"The Old Play House" also voices her protest against the male domination and the resultant humiliation:

> . . . Cowering
> Beneath your monstrous ego I ate the magic loaf and
> Became a dwarf. I lost my will and reason, to all your
> Questions I mumbled incoherent replies . . .
>
> (*The Old Playhouse,* 1)

The plight of a married woman, chained to her husband's house is depicted in the opening lines of the poem "The Old Play House":

> You planned to tame a swallow, to hold her
> In the long summer of your love so that she would forget
> Not the raw seasons alone, and the homes left behind,
>   but
> Also her nature, the urge to fly, and the endless
> Pathways of the sky. . .
>
> (*The Old Playhouse,* 1)

Kamala Das hates traditional sex roles assigned to women by the patriarchy. In the poem "Introduction" one finds resentment and refusal:

> . . . Then I wore a shirt
> and a black sarong, cut my hair short and ignored all of
> this womanliness. Dress in sarees, be girl or be wife,
> they cried. Be embroiderer, cook or a quarreller
> with servants.
>
> (*The Best of Kamala Das,* 12-13)

In the words of K. Satchidanandan, "The woman cannot change her body; so the poet changes her dress and tries to imitate men. But the voices of the tradition would force her back into sarees, the saree becoming here a sign of convention. She is pushed back into her expected gender roles: wife, cook, embroiderer quarreler with servants: the gender role also becomes a class role" (13).

The husband transforms the wife into the contemptible canine status of a housewife. To quote from the poem "Of Calcutta": "Here in my husband's home, I am a trained circus dog / Jumping my routine hoops each day." (*Collected Poems I,* 56-60)

Kamala Das is exclusively concerned with the personal experience of love in her poetry. "For her ideal love is the fulfilment of the levels of body and mind. It is the experience beyond sex through sex. The tragic failure to get love in terms of sexual-spiritual fulfilment from the husband leads her to search for it elsewhere. Each relationship only intensifies her disappointment faced with the sense of absolute frustration and loneliness" (Iyer, 203). Though she seeks the perfection of masculine being in every lover, it ends in failure because of the impossibility of realising this ideal in human form. The experience of frustration sets the psyche in the attitude of rebellion.

> I must pretend
> I must act the role
> Of happy woman
> Happy wife (*The Descendants,* p. 2) (qtd. in Iyer, 204)

Kamala Das's aim as a poet is to underline the predicament of contemporary women beset by the crisis of divided selves. She wants to bring harmony out of this existence. Her poems are remarkable because they reveal her feelings of anxiety, alienation, meaninglessness, futility, acute sense of isolation, fragmentation and loss of identity. Modern Indian woman's ambivalence is presented through her poems. She seems to have a good deal of the conventional woman in her. She seems to have the combination in herself—wish for domestic security and the desire for independence. Alongside her unfulfilled need for love there is the need to assert, to conquer and to dominate. While her poems describe a longing for a man to fill her dreams with love, she is also proud of her being the seducer, the collector especially of those men who pose as lady killers (Iyer, 193-194).

What strikes the reader most in her poetry is not the themes but the use of Indian English without concern for correctness and precision. "It appeared unpremeditated, a direct expression of feeling as it shifted erratica through unpredictable emotion, creating its own forms through its cadence and repetition of phrases, symbols and refrains. Her effort was to find an appropriate style for what is rather a poetry of a mind thinking about feeling than the expression of emotion" (Iyer, 194). Srinivasa Iyengar writes on her style: "While giving the impression of writing in haste, she reveals a mastery of phrase and a control over rhythm—the words often pointed and envenomed too, and the rhythm so nervously, almost feverishly alive. Her characteristic trick is to split phrases and meanings—even the infinitive—between two lines and this is surely symbolic of the fissured, or fractured, sensibility she wishes to communicate" (680).

It is thus proved that Kamala Das tried her best to uplift the position of woman and thus resist the dominance of man. The influence of patriarchy is found in all religions as well as their scriptures. As the religious leaders were all men, the scriptures written by them were male-oriented and as a result, women were given inferior position in families as well as societies. The religious leaders made their gods advice women, through the scriptures, to obey men. The Christian and Islamic religions do not treat men and women as equals. The women, in the roles of wives have to obey their husbands and be subservient to them. Thus this venomous ideology of male dominance is injected into even women's veins through the scriptures and they are destined to be inferior till they die.

In the Western society where religion's hold is loose, women enjoy more freedom and equality than the Eastern society. The very birth of Woman (Eve) in the *Bible* is patriarchal to the core. God made Eve out of Adam's rib. She was created for him to be his companion. Why did God create Man first instead of Woman who indeed bore and gave birth to offsprings? The influence of patriarchy is evident here. Again it was Eve who committed the sin first and then she tempted Adam to commit it. In reality is it woman who does more sexual outrages than man in any society?

Man has more muscular power than woman. At the same time woman has many qualities which man does not have. They should live in a harmony as other beings do around us. If man imitates other beings in sexual indulgence—overpowering the female—what differentiates human beings from other beings? Is our culture and civilisation leading us to barbarity? Even in this twentyfirst century women have no right to worship their Creator in mosques and some temples. This legacy of patriarchy has to be questioned. Women have every right to get out of their kitchens and houses and live equals to men. It is against this injustice in families and societies that feminists like Kamala Das fight against. Thus feminism seems to be an inevitable ideology, and more and more women have to come forward and fight for the women's cause. To sum up the article with a quotation from Srinivasa Iyengar:

> There is no doubt Kamala Das is a new phenomenon in Indo-Anglian poetry—a far cry indeed from Toru Dutt or even Sarojini Naidu. Kamala Das's is a fiercely feminine sensibility that dares without inhibitions to articulate the

> hurts it has received in an insensitive largely man-made world . . . Of course, the endless reiteration of such hurt, such disillusion, such cynicism, must sooner or later degenerate into a mannerism, but one hopes—and her exceptional talent offers the ground for such hopes—she will outgrow this obsession in due course and find her way to a season less trying than summer and a world other than the 'unreal' city of dreadful ghosts. (680)

Works Cited

Das, A Feminist Reading of Kamala Poetry Das, Kamala, *The Best of Kamala Das,* Ed. P. P. Raveendran, Calicut: Bodhi Publishing House, 1991.

Collected Poems I. Trivandrum: The Navakerala Printers, 1984.

My Story. New Delhi, Sterling Publishers, 1988.

The Old Playhouse and Other Poems, Mumbai, Orient Longman Private Limited, 1973.

Only the Soul Knows How to Sing, Kottayam, DC Books, 1996.

"Das, Kamala / Introduction." 18 October 2008 <http://www.enotes.com/poetry-criticism/das-kamala>.

"The Histrionics of Kamala Das." The Hindu 6 February 2000. 18 October 2008 <http://www.hinduonnet.com/2000/02/06/stories/1306078m.htm>.

Iyengar, K. R. Srinivasa, *Indian Writing in English,* New Delhi, Sterling Publishers Private Limited, 2001.

Iyer, N. Sharda, *Musings on Indian Writing in English, Volume 2 Poetry,* New Delhi, Sarup & Sons, 2005.

"Kamala Das." 18 October 2008 <http://www.sawnet.org/books/authors.php?Das+Kamala>.

Kumar, N. Prasantha, *Writing the Female: A Study of Kamala Das,* Kochi, Bharatiya Sahitya Pratishthan, 1998.

Raju, Dr. V. Alexander, "The Inevitable Metamorphosis: The Cocoon Breaks and 'Suraiya' Comes out of 'Kamala Das'", *Indian Journal of Postcolonial Literatures,* 2.1. (July 2001), 23-36.

Raveendran, Dr. N. V., "The Poems of Kamala Das: An Assessment" *Indian Writing in English,* Eds. Manmohan K. Bhatnagar and M. Rajeshwar, New Delhi, Atlantic Publishers and Distributors, 2000, 5-24.

Satchinandan, K., "Transcending the Body", *Only the Soul Knows How to Sing,* By Kamala Das. op.cit., 11-23.

3

Art and Aesthetic Vision in the Poetry of Kamala Das

— *Sheeba V. Issac*

Kamala Das is essentially a 'maker', a maker of meaning with words, a maker of order. Just as a designer might make a beautiful piece of furniture out of something as common as wood, so Kamala Das makes something original out of the ordinary materials of life and words. Her poetry goes beyond the traditionally accepted thought modes and embraces vast hidden areas of experience and complexity of feelings hitherto unexplored by other Indian women poets writing in English. Her poetry is not merely Indian like that of Toru Dutt and Sarojini Naidu, but a passionate expression of the universal experience of love, despair, anguish and failure apprehended through a feminine Indian sensibility. While Nissim Ezekiel and A.K. Ramanujan have preferred a cerebral, ironic and objective portrayal of life, Kamala Das tended to accord a greater significance to the life of feeling and contributed to the psychological and quasi-romantic dimensions and trends in modern Indian poetry in English.

Kamala Das is at her best a poet of private sensibility. Her consciousness is firmly yoked to the world around her, a world characterised by ecstasy and pain, love and despair. Her poems are gestures that counter the luridness of the world. Kamala Das's first volume of poems *Summer in Calcutta* (1965) arises from the poet's agonised response to the external world about the traumatic experiences of her childhood and early married life. The next collection *The Descendants* (1967) not only explores the leading motifs like love, lust and disillusionment, but also shows a metaphysical concern with time, death and decay. The *Old Playhouse and Other Poems* (1973) continues the poet's concern with the deeper meaning of life, death, disease and decay. In 1979, an unusual book entitled *Tonight, This Savage Rite* was published in which two major poets—Kamala Das and Pritish Nandy interacted in the common theme of love. In her *Collected Poems* (1984) we hear Kamala Das at her best with a more mature and sober poetic voice. Her latest poetry collection is published under the title, *Only the Soul Knows How to Sing* (1996).

It is difficult to determine where the artist begins in Kamala Das's poetry. Art is great, but greater far is life. Kamala Das seems to say that in order to accept art, one has to affirm sensuality. In her poems the meaning is found not in the poet's ideas but rather in the gap between her dream of order and the reality of life's lack of order. Kamala Das achieves poetic sublimity largely because of her pure aesthetic vision which is full of creativity and an awakened perception of poetic truth. The poetry of Kamala Das makes a discovery of many levels of paradoxes through which the self passes in order to define, authenticate and validate its total involvement in the affairs of life. The ultimate, mature vision unifies the self with the world outside. In the light of knowledge gained by the poet, external life becomes a macroscopic experience of inner life and inner life becomes a microscopic vision of the external life.

The artistic ability of Kamala Das is manifested in her technical skill in poetic composition. Form and content in her poetry are interdependent and constitute the indivisible core of poetic art. She chooses words by their tone of voice and uses them with unmistakable instinct to convey the perpetual burning within her. For her words are birds that take to wings with a bang as soon as the emotion or feeling takes shape out of the cauldron of experience. The confessional mode the poet has adopted aims at the recreation of intense feeling through a structure of words which expresses the turmoil of the self and evokes a responsive emotional disturbance in the reader. Felicity of expression, artistic ingenuity and dexterous craftsmanship exalt Kamala Das's poetic world to greater sublimity. Spontaneity and flow give her poetry a kind of lyrical and pictorial quality which is effective and touching.

There is a total fusion of thought, expression, rhythm and meaning in Kamala Das's verses and the words create a symbiosis of several sensations, visual, auditory and emotive. "The Freaks" opens with a visual image that claps on the reader's consciousness with sudden poetic impact.

> He talks, turning a sun-stained
> Check to me, his mouth, a dark
> Cavern, where stalactites of
> Uneven teeth gleam, his right
> Hand on my knee, [...] (1-5)

"Nani" begins with a direct, plain statement that, nevertheless, haunts the reader. "Nani the pregnant maid hanged herself / In the privy one day [...]" (1-2). "Herons" begins with the ironic and disturbing confession: "On sedatives / I am more lovable / Says my husband" (1-3). The abrupt and spontaneous beginning of "Summer in Calcutta" is striking and the words fall into a quick, evocative image:

> What is this drink but
> The April sun, squeezed
> Like an orange in
> My glass? I sip thee
> Fire? I drink and drink
> Again, I am drunk,
> Yes, but on the gold
> Of suns. [...] (1-8).

The word squeezed pervades the meaning of the poem.

Rhythm is an integral part of the meaning of a poem. Rhythmic sound has the ability to imitate the forms of physical behaviour and to express the complex and continuously shifting margin of human emotions. Both the free verse and the blank verse employed by Kamala Das are kept on bash by the discipline of rhythm and by the deft movement of lines. "A Request" is an example of rhythm harmonising with sense:

When I die
Do not throw
The meat and bones away
But pile them up
And let them tell
By their smell
What life was worth
On this earth
What love was worth
In the end.

The first line "When I die" balances with the last line "In the end". The expressions "meat and bones" and "pile them up" are positioned in harmonious order and the rhyming lines contribute to the overall rhythmic movement of the poem.

The powerful impression of the unity of thought and feeling and the unity of visual and auditory sensations that "The Dance of the Eunuchs" creates is primarily due to its excellent rhythmic / musical structure:

It was hot, so hot, before the eunuchs came
To dance, wide skirts going round and round, cymbals
Richly clashing, the anklets jingling, jingling
Jingling. Beneath the fiery gulmohur, with
Long braids flying, dark eyes flashing, they danced and
They danced, oh, they danced till they bled [...] (1-6)

Here words are like quicksilver carrying with them the sparkle of sense. In the sheer magic of rhythm and music and in the beauty of coalescing visual and auditory sensations, these lines are rarely surpassed in modern Indian poetry in English.

Kamala Das has never been obsessed with the intention of giving an Indian flavour to her language by deliberate manipulation. Nevertheless, Indian turns of phrases and nuances of Indian folk and poetic rhythms may be discovered in her poetry. However, great achievement lies in the deft manipulation of the foreign language of her choice to convey her moods and sensibility moulded by Indian ethos. She has not hesitated to use Indian expressions when occasion demands as in "In Love", "The White Flowers", "A Souvenir of Bone" and "The Ancient Mango Tree". She uses several phrases, expressions and even fragments of lines which would appear unidiomatic to a purist in language. The line "after / The drinks are drunk and the food eaten" (9-10) in "Death is so Mediocre" is a flavoured Indian expression, but effective. In 'The High Tide", the lines "The king's phone rings / Once, and it is a wrong number. What idiots, he says" (4-5) is purely Indian in tone. In "The Sea at Galle Face Green" two lines without verbs appear resembling vernacular usage: "No birdsong in the trees / Only the stomp of boots" (9-10).

One of the charges levelled against Kamala Das's poetic art is that it is devoid of humour and that her poetry is tense and taut in tone and there are not many light moments in it. Though satire and pun, quibble and banter are absent in her poetry, there is sensitive use of irony in several of her poems. Irony is a subtle device which involves stating the exact opposite of what is meant. Irony also arises from the contrast between the actual situation and what the situation ought to have been. In Kamala Das's poetry irony serves four purposes: it clarifies the theme and deepens the impact; it functions as a comment on social practices, situations and persons; it channelises rebelliousness and despair along civilised pathways of protest and finally it expresses a mature sense of resignation and compromise with the sorrows of the world.

The poem "Composition" has an ironic structure that enhances the significance of the theme.

> Husbands and wives,
> here is my advice to you.
> Obey each other's crazy commands,
> ignore the sane.
> Turn your home into a merry
> dog-house,
> marriage is meant to be all this
> anyway,
> being arranged in
> most humorous heaven. (191-200)

The ironic tenor of the passage is effectively clinched in the phrase "most humorous heaven."

Irony assumes a tinge of social criticism in the short poem "The Fancy Dress Show", as the poet exposes the great fancy dress show, that is, our civilisation.

Every virtue requires today
A fancy dress; the cassock is
The priest's main virtue, the clever
Politician dons a saint's mean
Apparel. (1-5)

The last two lines of the poem are a pungent adaption of Browning's famous couplet in "Pippa Passes" and give the poem a universal ironic dimension—"God is in his heaven and all / Is right with this stinking world" (15-16).

Imagery and symbols constitute the next most discernible powerful devices Kamala Das employs to mould her poetic art. While the impact of dramatic and narrative poetry depends on incidents, plot and character, in lyric poetry which is most personal, the poet achieves the effect through the employment of the figures of speech and figurative language. Imagery in poetry is the manner in which sensory responses are evoked through the representation of ideas of a collocation of words, conventional or unconventional. Imagery brings to the focus of our consciousness a sensory picture of experience, a recognisable image, a perceptible idea or notion by the deft combination of connotative words.

In "The Stone Age", Kamala Das evokes two striking images of lust in the following lines:

[...], ask me why his hand sways like a hooded snake
Before it clasps my pubis. Ask me why like
A great tree, felled, he slumps against my breasts,
And sleeps. [...] (19-22)

This is highly evocative erotic imagery. The "hooded snake" hides a phallic suggestion and reveals the poisonous nature of lust; the "great tree felled" indicates the repulsive exhaustion of the lover after the act of lust.

The imagery of the "trained circus dog" appears in more than one poem.

Yes, you came dear love, but late,
Late by thirty years or more, to the wrong place too;
Here in my husband's home I am a trained circus dog
Jumping my routine hoops each day, where is my soul,
My spirit, where the muted tongues of my desire?

("Of Calcutta", 92-6)

In "The Moon", the unchanging moon is identified as the circus dog: "[...] It is a trained circus dog / That shall never miss its hoop." (17-8). The imagery suggests a monotonous routine of life. One of the most evocative images in all Kamala Das's poetry appears in "The Dance of Eunuchs". The dance is picturised through words: "Long braids flying, dark eyes flashing, they danced and / They danced, [...]" (5-6). The ecstasy of the dance experience is rendered through an imagistic representation; the swaying and the heaving, the flush and the fire of the hot dance are galvanised into life. Kamala Das also employs brief verbal images that startle the reader into a consciousness of anguish and apprehension. The crows bickering over a piece of lizard meat on the old cannon stand ("The Testing of Sirens"), the sunshine lying near the door like a yellow cat ("The Sunshine Cat"), the "coiling snakes of silence" ("The Freaks", 17), and darkness lying behind the "bedroom door like a brooding / Dog" ("My Grandmother's House", 11-2) are images that enfold the convulsions of the poet's spirit.

A symbol is an objective image chosen to represent an abstraction because of an implied association of qualities or traits between the two. There are fixed symbols that acquire their meanings in the context if a given culture like "rose" for love or "serpent" for evil. There are also open-ended symbols representing a cluster of ideas and radiating diverse meanings like "sea" which may stand for life, immortality or a restless spirit. Kamala Das uses all types of symbols, though the open-ended type is more frequent. The sun and the sea are the two very pervasive symbols in Kamala Das's poetry. In her poetry the sun does not warm, it scorches. It is generally an oppressive symbol representing drabness, hostility and lust. At least once in "Ghanashyam" the sun is a warm and protective symbol when the poet addresses the Lord as "The cell of eternal sun, / The blood of the eternal fire, / The hue if the summer air" (51-3). Most of the poems in *Summer in Calcutta* ooze the summer heat and dust. In "The Conflagration" the lovers are two suns hot with the turbulence of passion. The sea is the most salutary and seminal symbol in her poetry. The sea was a part of her childhood consciousness as it was only two miles away from her ancestral home Nalapat. In "Composition" and in "The Suicide" the sea is the central symbol. The sea is the symbol of peace and spiritual detachment and the poet often wants to escape into its cool chambers. When despair grips her,

> All I want now
> is to take a long walk
> into the sea
> and lie there, resting,
> completely uninvolved.
> ("Composition", 233-7)

In "The Suicide", the poet converses with the sea and is momentarily taken in by the desire for death by merging with the sea.

> While I enter deeper,
> With joy I discover
> The sea's hostile cold
> Is after all skin-deep
> ("The Suicide", 56-9)

The symbols employed to show her nostalgia over the past glory are very touching. The neglect into which Nalapat house has fallen after death of the grandmother is touchingly described in "No Noon at My Village Home" and "Evening at the Old Nalapat House". The ghostly house and the death like silence of the place is symbolically expressed by the reference to owls, the cold pond, dust on window-sills, thatched trees and fireflies. Thus, the artful enlistment of artistic devices brings coherence and grace to Kamala Das's poetry.

A perfect poetic sublimity consists of five elements—grandeur of thought, capacity for strong emotion, appropriate use if figures, nobility of diction and finally harmonious composition. Out of these five elements, two, namely high thinking which implies the power to form great conceptions and high feeling which means vehement and inspired passion, depend on the nature of poetic vision. The rest three are entirely subservient to technical skill generating artistic impact. In the poetry of Kamala Das high thinking and high feeling combine together to impart supreme aesthetic delight. Kamala Das's aesthetic experience is a combination of strong cathartic import dormant in her confessional autobiographical poetry, full of creativity and an awakened perception of poetic truth which spreads its wings to a kind of yoga or meditation, grooming or cultivation, spiritual evolution or creative process.

Cathartic effect ends in providing "rasa", which Vyasa Muni considers to be the soul, the essence of poetry. It has been said in the Upanishads that the "rasa" is Brahma Himself. "Rasa" is said to be the soul of Indian poetics and it has gradually come to be accepted as the soul of Indian aesthetics and aesthetic experience. For old pedagogues like Bharata and Bhamaha, and also for celebrated men of learning like Acharya Dhananjaya, "rasa" is closely connected to the poetic vision. While dealing with the cathartic effect in his *Poetics,* Aristotle regards the most perfect tragic pleasure as possible only through the purgation of the feelings of pity and fear. In fact, catharsis is a process of learning, and therefore, pleasurable. The more and intense the poetic sensibilities are, the more powerful will be the poetic sublimity or aesthetic experience. Confessional poetry of Kamala Das has been inferred to be associated with cathartic effects and intense feminine sensibilities.

Like all confessional poets, Kamala Das gives literary form a new sense of personality, attaching value to the image of man. She raises her confessional traits to the level of a specific universal appeal. The struggle of oneself ultimately becomes the struggle of the whole humanity. Because of absolute confessions made by a group of poets in their poetry, particularly in America, such poets as Robert Rowell, Theodore Roethke, Anne Sexton, Sylvia Plath and John Berryman have raised themselves to a level known as confessional poets and Kamala Das's place is certainly secure in the ranks of these poets.

Kamala Das's own traumatic experiences in love and in sex are candidly confessional and absolutely forthright. She does not hide her own bodily changes, joys and failures in love and sex and her own attitude towards her husband / lover. In a poignant articulated tone, she writes,

> [...] I was a child, and later they
> Told me I grew, for I became tall, my limbs
> Swelled and one or two places sprouted hair. When

I asked for love, not knowing what else to ask
For, he drew a youth of sixteen into the
Bedroom and closed the door. He did not beat me
But my sad woman-body felt so beaten
The weight of my breasts and womb crushed me. [...]

("An Introduction", 23-30)

Kamala Das openly revolts against the traditionally accepted, strange, queer womanhood concepts in the Indian society, which is so awkwardly full of abominable shams and cants. Rigid trammels of tyranny, she does not like at all. In a bitter, piercing cathartic tone, Kamala Das ridicules traditional imposters, show of masculine strength and also man's lust:

[...] you were pleased
With my body's response, its weather, its usual shallow
Convulsions. You dribbled spittle into my mouth. You
poured
Yourself into every nook and cranny, you embalmed
My poor lust with your bitter sweet juices [...]

("The Old Playhouse", 8-12)

Her confessions are tall, far-reaching and meaningful. Frequently, they verge on the point of revolution in the poetic world.

Kamala Das's poetry is a valid standard in aesthetic appreciation since it is sufficiently subtle and complex to embrace the varieties of human life. Her four volumes of poems express the simple, tender and serious emotions which have a universal appeal. Her poems are full of life's themes.

The title poem "Summer in Calcutta" derives its poetic and aesthetic meaning from the poet's intimacy with the torture of Indian summer. The April sun brings a sense of sensuous repletion and warm intoxication. The poet is drunk on the gold of suns. The first line of the poem is related to the last forming a single line "What is this drink but juice of April suns" making the poem a circumscribed experience of heat, intoxication, sensuousness and laughter. The question

What is drink but
The April sun, squeezed
Like an orange in
My glass? (1-4)

sets forth the tone of the poem. The April sun becomes the "noble venom" that flows through the poet's veins providing a temporary triumph over life's despairs. Just as the sun is transformed into a juice, heat is transferred into laughter; despair is transformed into hopeful desire. The significance of the poem lies not in its evocation of heat and sweat but in its instillation of a regenerate mood of sensuality and passion through the absorption of sensuousness.

In "Winter" the sense of physical warmth and well-being is placed against the bitter cold of winter winds. "A Relationship" identifies love with physical desire. In "The Testing of the Sirens" the poet wakes from a night of love and lust into a morning heavy with a sense of loneliness. The poem is a part of that endless search for an eternal and perfect lover which is one of the central themes in all Kamala Das's poetry. Here love becomes an endless and painful experiment for possession. The evasiveness of real love and the cruelty of lust posing as love are brought out in the two images of the pregnant girl baring her dusky breasts and the crows bickering over a piece of lizard meat.

"I shall Some Day" is an amalgam of defiant hope and freakish desire. The poem is addressed to the husband. The theme is the intense desire of the woman to break loose from the cocoon of false love and tired lust. In "The Fear of the Year" the poet is concerned with the cruelty of time that does not yield to the fascinations of love: "For no smile, however fond, can / Settle time like a paper weight" (4-5).

Kamala Das's high thinking is reflected in certain poems, for example, "The Siesta" is symbolic of the progress of the self from the state of dream to that of wakefulness. Sleep is the sunlit tank that enfolds the dream of life. In the hostile depth of the tank there is disturbance (turtles and eels). The libido is tortured. Slowly the poet wakes into consciousness.

> But as evening comes
> snake-like she sheds
> their silver coils and wakes
> to meet this alien world which talks
> of Gods and casual sins (10-4).

The poem suggests that in the last stage of life one wakes into a better understanding about the meaning of existence, God and sin.

A poem more popular than any other in Summer in Calcutta is "An Introduction" variously interpreted and applauded as intensely auto-biographical and as the poet's aesthetic manifesto. It has an amazingly prosaic beginning with a reference to politics to which the poet is indifferent. Then it moves on to Kamala Das's credo about poetic language and finally it forays into some autobiographical references and experiences. "An Introduction" is an attempt to assert the poet's individuality and feminine identity against social and cultural conformity. However, the attempt is dissipated to a large extent due to the intrusion of extraneous sensibilities. The poem adopts a conversational tone and rhythm throughout; its short lines indicate an abrupt and annoyed reaction to the burdens of growth.

In "Forest Fire", the theme is the self trying to engulf the whole world:

> [...] In me the street-lamps
> Shall glimmer, the cabaret girls cavort, the
> Wedding drums resound, the eunuchs swirl coloured
> Skirts and sing sad songs of love, [...] (17-20)

The awareness of the universality of the self is, once again revealed in "Someone Else's Song". The poet's self goes out in sympathy to identify itself with the voices, sufferings and travails of the millions around her. An empathy with the fate of others, their births and deaths, silences and sufferings forms the central strain of the poem. The same spiritual truth of the self binds together the mysterious variety of forms and formations in the universe.

"The Descendants" shows a metaphysical concern with time, death and decay. It reveals the thematic and symbolic structure of a poetic consciousness moulded by meditation over death and physical decay, ugliness of the body and the mind, and the fallibility of human emotions. A preoccupation with loneliness and a corroding sense of futility mark some of the poems. The incongruity between man's guiding desires and the insubstantiality of his achievements strikes the poet lending her vision of human destiny a tragic dimension.

"The Looking Glass" is about man-woman relationship, love and lust. There is an ironic suggestion about the need to flatter the male ego. There is unrelieved sense of despair in the thought that in spite of the sacrifices and self-effacement of woman, it is difficult to keep the man with her. He slips away insulting the woman's pleasure of possession. The painful contradiction in the man-woman relationship is brought out:

> [...] Oh, yes, getting
> A man to love is easy, but living
> Without him afterward may have to be
> Faced. [...] (16-9)

"Composition" is one of the longer poems of Kamala Das in which the thematic intensity sometimes flags because of its sheer length. "The White Flowers" and "Jaisurya" are poems conceived in a different mould from the rest in *The Descendants.* In the former there is thoughtfully expressed anxiety and anguish—war destroys both love and life. The poet's concern for her baby-son born in an age of bloodshed and despair grows into a universal concern for mankind. The latter is one of the most acutely personal poems of Kamala Das. It is a narrative meditation on childbirth.

In the early poems, Kamala Das is mainly obsessed with her own restlessness and agony in the face of the male turbulence. However, the growing diversity of her poetic vision and maturity of response to the milieu are seen in some of the poems dealing with social and interpersonal themes in *The Old Playhouse and Other Poems.* "The Inheritance" is such a poem inspired by the poet's disgust with everyday religion. We have grown scabrous and our "fathers' lunacy" speaks through our thoughts and actions.

The poems in *Tonight, This Savage Rite* are a testimony to Kamala Das's remarkable ability to transform sensuality and sexual frustration into lyric expressions of touching aesthetic beauty. Several facets of love-experience from the sensual to the spiritual are caught at their climatic points. Love's myriad moments of delight and suffering are recollected and recorded into a puzzling pattern of intense experience and a structure of feeling.

Kamala Das is not a social analyst; she does not suggest remedies; she is not even a social satirist as Nissim Ezekiel is in some of his poems. She focuses attention on the dehumanising effect of social injustice and inequality and on the deterioration of human psyche under the impact of social and moral conventions. Thus, her aesthetic vision not only encompasses high thinking and high feeling but also shows a social, universal, personal and above all psychological tinge of originality. That imparts "rasa" in its supreme sublimity of spiritual realisation.

Thus, it is this two distinguishing features of Kamala Das's poetry— her art and aesthetic vision— that thrusts into the consciousness of the reader the private pleasures and nightmares of the poet in a realistic manner. Writing, to Kamala Das is an appetite, a psychic necessity, a spiritual hunger, a biological drive to write away the loneliness and betrayal. An attempt to achieve a sense of completeness through writing and to relive the imperfectly lived or half-lived moments of life bears testimony to her unifying and unified vision of life as a literary artist.

Works Cited

Das, Bijay Kumar, *A Reader's Guide to Ten Twentieth Century Indian Poets,* Bareilly, Prakash, 1993.

Das, Kamala, *Kamala Das: The Old Playhouse and Other Poems,* Madras, Orient Longman, 1973.

— *Collected Poems,* Trivandrum, Navakerala, 1984.

— *Only the Soul Knows How to Sing,* Kottayam, DC, 1996.

Dharwadker, Vinay, and A.K. Ramanujan, eds., *The Oxford Anthology of Modern Indian Poetry,* Delhi, Oxford UP, 1994.

Gokak, Vinayak Krishna, ed., *The Golden Treasury of Indo-Anglian Poetry,* New Delhi, Sahithya Akademi, 1970.

Kaur, Iqbal, ed., *Perspectives on Kamala Das's Poetry,* New Delhi, Intellectual, 1995.

Naik, M.K., *A History of Indian English Literature,* Delhi, Sahithya Akademi, 1982.

Narasimhaiah , C.D., ed., *Makers of Indian English Literature,* Delhi, Pencraft International, 2000.

Parthasarathy, R., ed., *Ten Twentieth Century Indian Poets,* Delhi, Oxford UP, 1976.

Peerardina, Saleem, ed., *Contemporary Indian Poetry in English: An Assessment and Selection.* Madras, Macmillan, 1972.

Taru, Susie, and K.Lalita, eds., *Women Writing in India,* New Delhi, Oxford UP, 1993.

4

Paradigm and Politics of Conversion: The Case of Kamala Suraiya

— Neeru Tandon

While returning from a very enjoyable and meaningful seminar from Haridwar I came to know from a very dear friend of mine about the case of the son of Haryana's seasoned politician Bhajan Lal, who decided to convert to Islam. The conversion was apparently not because of his strong faith but for getting married for the second time. So Chandra Mohan became Chand Mohammed and his lady love, lawyer and former Assistant Advocate General Anuradha Bali appeared as Fiza. I found it to be an abuse of the system and religion. Just like actor Dharmendra who married Hema Malini, and many others in public life who become Muslims just to get married for the second time and avoid legal hassles as the Hindu law doesn't permit such marriages.

It reminded me of a very frank, bold and controversial Indian English poet Kamala Das, who at the age of 67, converted to Muslim in 1999 (on Dec. 11, to be precise) and adopted the name Kamala Suraiya. She was short listed for the Nobel Prize for literature in 1984 along with Margnirit Yourcevior, Doris Lessing and Nadine Gordimer. The term CONVERSION evokes a dramatic appeal that suggests suddenness, although in most cases it implies a gradual process of establishing and defining a new religious identity. Although rarely treated as a cultural phenomenon, conversions can obviously be examined with reference to the norms, values and presuppositions of the cultures in which they take place. Thus politics of conversion raises many questions. Before we trace the idea of conversion in the life and poetry of Kamala Das, it would be proper to pause and consider conversion as such.

Much of it is hidden in the recent rise of Hinduism as an aggressive political response to monotheist faiths. Historically, Hinduism suffered in the case of conversion to Islam or Christianity. When Islam invaded India, scheduled caste Hindus, specially in Bengal, embraced it as boon against the tyranny of Brahmanism. However, Islamic rule didn't create much of a communal tension because a majority of Muslim leaders were also supporter of caste based Hindu system and indeed, Indian version of Islam adopted its neo casteism by attaching the elites to superior ethnicity to distinguish themselves from local low caste Hindu converts. Except for Aurangzeb, who was an Islamic zealot, a very high degree of cohesion between Hindus and Muslims can be found throughout the entire Islamic history of India.

On the other hand, when Christian missionaries came to India, they too found their soft targets in scheduled caste Hindus (case of Bakha in M.R.Anand's *Untouchable*) during sixteenth and seventeenth centuries. However, they faced a daunting task of conversion because by then Hindus were aware that lower castes may leave Hindu society altogether and also that conversion is not a complete readymade solution for them. Nevertheless success of Christian missionaries in terms of conversion was very limited and they established themselves by social service to common mass in the form of convents, charitable hospitals and missionaries. But it cannot be denied that the ambiguity and sometimes ruthless denial of human position of lower caste in Hinduism made them vulnerable to conversion. The position of women in some traditional and conservative houses was no different. In most of the Hindu families women were always taught to regard themselves as beings who were eventually to be married off and have children and serve the husband whether he was kind and desirable or not. In addition to all this, men in Hinduism were treated literally as almost gods or semi-gods.

The above point is a connecting link between these facts and the case of Kamala Suraiya Das. When asked what lured her to Islam, she gave two plain reasons. One is the purdah; the other is the security that Islam provides to women. In fact, both the reasons are complementary but illogical.

Let us see this conversion of Hindu Kamala Das to Muslim Kamala Suraiya first from her own point of view as stated in various interviews by her. She has sent shock waves, this time not through a sex-oozing autobiography (*My Story*) or nude paintings but by becoming a neophyte after the death of her husband Madhavdas.

We know, Kamala Das belongs to that generation of post-independence women poets who have given a convinced assurance that Indian English poetry matches the best anywhere. Melanie Silgardo, Sujata Bhatt, Eunice de Souza, Mamta Kalia, Tara Patel, Imtiaz Dharker etc. make the group, and Kamala Das obviously and rightly has a proud claim to be among them. She has not only broadened the thematic concerns of Indian English poetry but has also shown how words and images can recreate lived experiences, express the anguish and pain and at the same time give a new outlook to the world regarding the feminine psyche. Her poetry, fiction, autobiography, painting and short stories along with her columns reflect and depict her deeply sensitive and keenly insightful understanding and response to culture. She picked up threads from most simple things, weaving them into exquisite moments. Her sincerity and frankness in handling the issues of social, cultural and religious significance sensitised the readers equally well. No Malayalam writer –living or dead—wrote as beautifully as she did. Her biographer, Merrily Weisbord, calls her a true poet.

Kamala Das began to write at the age of six. She has the perfection both in prose and verse. She wrote effectively in both the languages, English and Malayalam. She has also held the position of vice-chairperson in Kerala Sahitya Academy. The language she uses is chiselled, filtered and transparent. The prolific writer M.T. Vasudevan Nair paid rich tributes to her when he said if someone made him jealous by the mastery over language, it was Madhavikutty.

Kamala Das's decision to use English as a language of writing poetry is not only influenced by education but also by the poor state of regional language poetry. When she began writing in English there was no modern poetry in Malayalam. That is the reason why many poets have been particularly active in translating from regional languages. When Kamala Das wished to begin writing poetry (as she has inherited it from her mother and uncle) her husband supported the decision. However she could not enjoy the morning-till-night schedule like her great uncle. To accept poetry writing as the fullfledged work was difficult for her. She had to wait till night to write. In an interview, she accepts; "There was only the kitchen table where I could cut vegetables and after all the plates and things were cleared, I would sit there and start typing."

Kamala Das has always been daring and forthright. She has criticised the traditionbound, conservative society which of course was always harsh on her unconventional lifestyle. She received accolades and many awards for her literary contributions like Asian Poetry Prize, Kent Award for English writing from Asian Countries, Asian World Prize, Sahitya Academy Award, Kerala Sahitya Academy Award, etc. Her autobiography *My Story* was a huge success and has been published in more than 15 languages. It is now a school textbook in Japan and Canada. Kamala Das lived with the passion of an undaunted rebel .The intensity and eloquence of her life and her poetic accomplishments have dumbfounded the male chauvinists and have left her female counterparts in soaring spirits. She confirms our convictions that socio- cultural and socio-religious restrictions on women have robbed them of all their potentialities leaving them not only physically and mentally handicapped but also psychological wrecked age after age.

The life experiences of Kamala Das have been honestly expressed in her poetry with the courage of conviction. Her humanistic and feministic concerns with her anguish and agony, sympathy and protest convey the message silently, though its explosive power has been felt by everyone. No wonder her rebellion has caused a flutter in the socalled 'guardians of orthodox religions, custodians of culture and pettifogging politicians.' Controversies have always dogged the writer, who created a storm when she published her autobiography *My Story* and presented her painting of nude female body to the world.

Her husband's homosexual tendencies that drove her to don a male attire to lure him induced certains things in her which could give birth to a rebel. Her search for an identity became more difficult with such superimposed conceptions of an ideal in different roles. Should she behave like a wife who can rightfully claim her husband's love or seduce in masculine garb, should she exhibit her natural feminity or enforced masculinity? All these created a bewildering schizophrenia in her. I personally feel that her work is important, very important; precisely it presents truth, a different kind of truth, which people find difficult to discuss and digest.

Kamala Das had come to Kerala from Kolkata during the 1980's. She first settled in the state capital Thiruvananthapuram and shifted to Kochi a few years later to be with her poetess mother Balamani Amma. Her decision to hand over her ancestral property at Punnayurkulum to the Kerala Sahitya Academi also drew publicity agents. I agree with the celebrated novelist, Namita Gokhale who says that "her persona overtook her writing in public mind." Here in this paper I am not talking about Kamala Das's poetry, novel or short stories. My concentration is on her conversion from Kamala Das to Kamala Suraiya. In an interview known as "The Rediff Interview with Shobha Warrier", she said, "I went on experimenting with painting, poetry, fiction, drama I am also a columnist I think I have become a professional writer as it is difficult remaining a poet because poetry doesn't sell in this country." She further added, "I wanted to fill my life with as many experiences as I can manage to garner because I do not believe that one can get born again." When she released the first nude painting in 1980s made by her, she proclaimed, "I find the nude female body the most beautiful in the word." Ironically the same woman adopted Islam, and left Hinduism to have security through Islamic purdah or burqua.

Many times she admitted that she always wanted love and when she didn't get it within her home she tried to stray a little. She admitted that she was being unfaithful to her spouse because she did not get love from her husband.

My point is that the same thing can be applied to her case of conversion as well. When she was not satisfied from her husband she went for extra-marital relationships, in the same way when she was not comfortable with Hindu religious practices, she converted herself to Muslim at the age of 67. On December 11, 1999 it was at a public seminar that Kamala Das announced her conversion to Islam publicly. Now Kamala Das and Madhavikutty will be known as Suraiya, meaning a splendid star. She says, "Yes, the controversial Madhavikutty is dead. This is the last time I am shocking you all."

Das argued that purdah in Islam is the most wonderful dress for women in the world. She had always loved to wear it as it gives women a sense of security. About her conversion to Islam she told that she had been lonely all through her life. But she was no longer a loner. Islam was her company. According to her Islam is the only religion in the world that gives love and protection to women. I quote:

> At night I sleep holding a pillow close to me. I am all alone. But now it seems I have many with me. There is no religion like Islam that protects women. At this age, that is what I need. The most merciful will provide me care and protection. Therefore I have converted.

She shifted all the Hindu idols in her home, including her intimate friend and love, Lord Krishna, to the guestroom. Saying namaaz five times a day has become a regular feature. Her formal initiation into Islam took place in front of the Muslim clergy at Palayam Mosque in Thiruvananthapuram.

We know that purdah (burqua) is associated with Muslim women only, although in parts of Indian society also, purdah is observed and the tradition adhered to in the same spirit of social and cultural prescription. Kamala Suraiya shifted her house, her way of living and even her faith. Her multi-coloured sarees have given way to the single-coloured burqua. The red mark on the forehead (bindi) also vanished away. She has become a student again, started learning Muslim culture. A Muslim girl has started giving her lessons in Arabic.

She has many arguments in support of her conversion. For her, conversion to Islam arose out of conviction and was not a sudden decision. She says the 'idea' to convert had been there in her mind for the last three decades. It has been churning in her mind. According to newspapers for many days prior to her formal announcement in this regard, she had been meeting Muslim religious scholars and women members of the community in Malappuram, the state's pre-dominant Muslim district. Some comments by her are very vital in this regard. I quote, "I kept my desire a secret for long. But now the time has come when I can no longer remain a Hindu. I hate being cremated as a Hindu. I love being buried as a Muslim." She doesn't care whether her decision has shocked her friends and other Malayalees or not. She says, "I don't care I always believe I am what I am, enough is enough in Hinduism." She further says, "No religion can restrict me. I am always myself. I love being Muslim now. I will start writing poems and prose on Allah and Islam. Allah will henceforth inspire my creativity whether it is poetry or paintings." (MG-The Milli Gazette Indian Muslims Leading English Newspaper: Suraiya: Search for Redemption, A.G.Khan).

Kamala Das's embracing of Islam has caused consternation to some, while the Hindus are shunned by the reasons she enumerated. She was uncomfortable with Hinduism and Hindu gods. She said that Hindus have abused and hurt her. They have often tried to scandalise her. "I cannot repose faith in Hinduism because Hindu gods never forgive, they only punish," she fumes. She thought that she won't be forced to make compromises in her new religion and Islam will tolerate her controversial past. She says, "Religion cannot claim one's creativity. Islam is tolerant. Allah is the god of love and forgiveness. My mind tells me Allah has forgiven me, my sins, if they were sins."

It is quite surprising that a person of high literary calibre like Kamala Das who hails from an intellectual Hindu background was absolutely ignorant of the essence of her ancestral Vedic wisdom that penetrated into various aspects of human understanding. If she is not deliberately ignorant of her great grandpa's asset Lord Krishna has a cure for her obsession in *Srimad Bhagavad Gita,* which is known as the unsectarian theology for the entire mankind. I quote one from the granth for Suraiya's burden of carrying gods.

> *The devotees who worship other deities with deep faith are worshipping me alone (G, 9:25).*

The one-God theory is profusely found in the *Vedas* and their various branches. She is the same who sometimes is so engrossed in Lord Krishna that claims her complete surrender, while sometimes she sees the image of Bala Gopal Krishna in her little son. In *My Story* she writes", "I filled his (her son's) childhood with magic and wonder... He sat on my knee looking like the infant Krishna." (*My Story*, p.114)

She feels that poet's own personality is the raw material for his or her poetry. Her thoughts, her poems, her autobiography all confirm her unflinching devotion to Lord Krishna. Such passages are numerous in her autobiography. Her devotion to Lord Krishna has eventually made her happy and contented. I quote from her autobiography, "Free from that lust of human bondage, I turned to Krishna. In the old playhouse of my mind, in its echoing hollowness. His voice was sweet. He had come to claim me ultimately. Therefore he dwelt in my dreams. Often I sat cross-legged before a lamp reciting mantras in his praise." (p.195)

The surreptitious confession of her love for Krishna becomes a passionately blatant assertion in 'Ghanshyam'. Let us see some lines from her poetic world:

> Ghanshyam
> You have like a koel built your nest
> In the harbour of my heart
> My life until now a sleeping
> Jungle is at last astir with music
> You lead me along a route,
> I have never known before.
> And one more example
> O Shyam, My Ghanshyam
> With words. I weave a raiment (clothing) for you
> With songs a sky
> With such songs I liberate
> In the oceans then fervid dance.

The 'Oceans' refer to the subconscious mind which responds with 'fervid dance' to the music of praise, while the raiment of words and the sky of song, connoting the conscious state and the super-conscious levels respectively, suggests a total involvement in the act of adoring the lord.

> Shyam, O Ghanshyam
> You have like a fisherman cast
> your net in the narrows
> of my mind

And towards you my thought today
Must race like enchanted fish...

At this point it might perhaps be appropriate to mention severt important poems that deal specifically with Radha's love for Krishan for using this traditional love as symbols of the soul's quest and confluence (an act of merging, junction of two rivers) with the divine, the poet reveals the fulfilment attained through uninhibited surrender the poems in question are 'Radha Krishna', 'Radha', The Maggots', 'A Phantom-Lords', 'Sunset', 'Blue-Bird', 'The Blind Walk' and 'The Paper-Moon'.

The comment of P.Malikarjuna Rao in this regard needs attention. I quote:

> But in Kamala Das the element of bhakti is absent. Her relation with Krishna is purely human. She confesses, 'I was looking for an ideal lover. I was looking for the one who went to Mathura and forgot to return to his Radha.' (p.59)

I feel she has just given a mythical framework to her search for true love, and tries to identify it with Radha-Krishna myth or with Mira Bai's relinquishing of her, of marriage in search of Lord Krishna, the true lover. She says: "Vrindavan lives on in every woman's mind, and the flute luring her from house and her husband". (*My Story*, p.27-28)

If one tries to find the religious sentiments and goes deep into her poetry, one can easily find that true peace and tranquillity of the soul are not evident in her poems. On the contrary the awareness of that peace which comes with the soul's union with the Divine as in the Radha-Krishna poems remains a far-off vision that she is trying to reach through the theories of physical frustration. What causes amazement to me is that a sensitive person like poetess Kamala Das , who sings songs of divine love, who celebrates love of Radha-Krishan and considers herself as the true devotee of Ghanshyam, all of sudden takes them just as idols; and transfers them from temple to drawing-room as showpieces. Isn't it surprising and shocking?

It's anyone's right to convert to any religion, but the way the writer had done that is not worth of her calibre. Suddenly overnight posing in a praying posture or wearing a purdah; all seemed like public gimmick only. No wonder, people blame her for embracing Islam for cheap publicity and some personal benefits.

Her friends disclose two entirely different reasons for her allurement to convert to Islam. One, she was in love with a Muslim whom she was expecting to marry. Secondly she wanted to join politics. It was also the news that she wanted to please filmmaker Ismail Merchant who is reportedly making a film based on her controversial autobiography *My Story*. Less than a year later Kamala Suraiya announced her plans to register her political party 'Lok Seva' (rediff on the net, Dec. 14, 1999).

When enquired, Surayya agrees and disagrees. It is said, "It is true that I am in love. I am in love with a person. Only four persons know my mobile number. My three sons and my lover. I plan to marry him in six months." She does not disclose whether her lover is a Muslim or not. She refutes the rumour that Merchant is making a film on her. According to her it is not Merchant but the Canadian director Arvi Galbert who was going to make a film on her life.

We are aware of Kamala Das's love for politics. In the 1970's Keralites saw Kamala Das enter politics with a campaign for an indigenous green movement. She contested the assembly elections, traversing the countryside, asking for votes from the people in the villages and Muslim areas. She lost, but that did not deter her from involving herslef in politics. The Kerala Assembly Election 2006 again had Kamala Surayya's involvement. On 28 April 2006, local newspaper published from Kochi tells us that the noted writer Kamala Suraiya, who came out in support of LDF supported independent candidate, K.T. Jaleel at Kuttppuram, has received threats to her life, following which she has been given police protection. Surayya had in an interview to a local newspaper supported K.T. Jaleel, contesting former industries Minister, P.K. Kunhalikutty at Kultipuram.

Though Kamala Das is not the only one to accept conversion yet her sopporters find it difficult to accept it wholeheartedly. Muslims and Hindu are equally against such conversions. The influential Ludhiana Jama Masjid's Shahi Imam Habibur Rahman Savi Ludianvi has issued a fatwa against conversion and people like Fiza and Chand Mohd., and termed the wedlock as a fraud.

Very soon, Chand Mohd. deserted Fiza alias Anuradha and went back to his first wife and family. Kamala's case and its result are not much different.

The scene changes and in 2006, after the elections, Kamala Das issued a statement at a book releasing ceremony orgainised by Kairali books in Kochi that she deeply regrets converting to Islam and is disillusioned with the treacherous behaviour of her Muslim friends. She claims that all wealth amounting to several lakhs, gold ornaments, books and other valuables have been looted by Muslims. Even in an interview with noted writer Tasleema Nasreen she exhibited her depression and discontement regarding conversion to Islam. But she cannot revert. Among the converts to Islam, a few do take the difficult step of renouncing their faith in Islam and reverting to Hinduism as it is clear that apostasy (abandoning Islam) is punishable by death.

Like most Indians I also value all religions but what I find objectionable is that Suraiya's explaination of equating the purdah with Islam is limiting a great religion to a dress code. The whole life, for 66 long years, she felt secure, having marital and extra-marital relations, painting her nude female body and writing poems about male-female relations. But at the age of 67 she feels insecure and according to her only Islam can give her that security. Is it believable? She has justified the Muslim's right to four wives. She views this archaic practice as a generous gesture—where a man gives 'life' to four women. In reality she still lives with her 'Kafir' (non-Muslim) son at Pune. By seeking non-Islamic protection of her own kafir son, Kamala Suraiya has once again denounced Islam and Allah. (Why I say this will be evident from *Quran* 9:23 and 58:22). The *Quran* strictly warns the Muslims not to develop any relationship with the non-Muslims even if they are their close kith and kin. It goes like this: "Believers do not believe your father or brothers if they prefer other religions (unbelief) in preference to Islam. The Muslims who associate with the non-Muslims are wrong doers and great is their punishment."

The feminists are blowing hot and cold to see the crusader and champions of women's liberation advocating purdah. She had advocated burqah as a 'bullet-proof' dress. Her choice of Islam comes as a stunning blow to those who regard Islam too suffocating for women. She has always been something of a cult figure in Kerala. Women with literary aspirations still hope to write like her. In that sense her private life cannot be completely separated from her public sphere. Her conversion and adopting purdah benefited many. A crop of purdah shops named after Suraiya, alias Madhavikutty, alias Kamala Das, has sprung up in several towns of Malabar in the wake of her hyped-up conversion to Islam, like 'Suraiya Purdah Houses', 'Suraiya Purdha Palaces' and 'Suraiya Purdah Paradises' (Malappuram, April 12, 2000- *The Hindu*- on line edition) Thursday, April 13, 2000).

Many of the 'Suraiya' shops are just old wine in a new bottle, a marketing strategy by which they simply changed their names to cash in on the endorsement of the attire by the celebrity writer. The picture of Kamala Suraiya bearing out of a black purdah had appeared in newspapers and magazines of Kerala. Her endorsement was godsend to religious revivalists as well as purdah firms that mushroomed in the Malabar region in the mid-1990s. When asked just after conversion Kamala says, "I am very happy to know that there are purdah shops in my name. I feel like jumping up and down like a child. I love the Purdah."

Kamala Das, who was always after publicity, and pleasure became a hellcat for some, due to her promiscuous relations. "More often than not she concentrates on sexual love", (21) ..... "Again and again, she resorts to 'I', and 'My' and 'mine'. What can be a stronger proof of her subjectivism' than this?" (44) (A.N.Dwivedi).

Educated Muslims are also against her conversion. Prof Hameed Chennamangallor has warned that her remarks would 'promote' reactionary tendencies in the community, and that "they would lead to legitimising the Purdah and polygamy." Mr. Anakkayam Syed Mohammed, a rationalist and Ms. V.P.Zuhre, a women's activist, feel the Maverick (independentminded person, unorthodox) poet's remarks would "check the effect to emancipate Muslim women".

Paradigm and politics of conversion from one religion to another, especially by public figures, does create disharmony in society. Religion is a matter of faith and lifelong practice. Just a particular dress-code or some different 'puja-practices' cannot make you a different person. I admire Kamala Das's belief that tradition, ideology, customs and beliefs may be changed or discarded, if they have gone beyond the expiry date and seem useless. It is essential to mention that she looked after two Muslim children and said, "It was an emotional experiment. I wanted to know whether I could love them. And I could."

Whether the conversion was spiritually inspired or matrimonially motivated (like Fiza and Chand Mohd.) at the age of 67 is a fact still to be established. There are many ways of looking at Kamala Das's conversion to Islam. For some, the fact that an upper caste woman can convert to a minority religion is evidence of a commendable courage albeit one tinged with eccentricity. Especially now, when a strong anti-conversion drive has been launched by certain extremist Hindu groups. But then that is Kamala Das all over again. All her life she has enjoyed defying taboos. Certainly her action has electrified Kerala's somewhat moribund social scene. Whether her change of heart is hormonal or spiritual, her decision to marry (which didn't take place) and to adopt a new religion, expose new realms of a faith in a particular religion and pose many debatable questions yet to be answered.

5

Confession of Mutilation and Sufferings of Women

(A Study of the Selected Poems by Kamala Das)

— Masoumeh M. Moradi

Born on March 31, 1934 in Malabar in Kerala, Kamala Das is very well recognised as one of India's foremost poets. She is a poet of many facets and moods.

From the beginning Kamala Das demonstrates a continuity of theme and expression concerning central division of the self. Her work is a compelling account of the presence of split. She speaks out her heart on her own premises. She redefines herself and liberates herself both as a woman and a poet. She struggles to cope with her problems and dilemmas. She does not attempt to intellectualise nor does she attempts to spiritualise. She makes a discovery of human existence and narrates her experiences vividly and passionately. She protests against the marginalisation of women and social injustices and communicates a powerful female sensibility in her poetry.

An analysis of her poems reveal that the woman persona of her poems represent her 'own mutilated self' tormented by both past and present, and resulting in deep sense of crisis. She feels exploited and cheated by the civilisation of which she is a part. She seems to find no way out of her tormented inner world and knows that there can be no easy solution

Issues concerning women are the recurring themes in the volumes of Kamala Das. Women's social unrest in respect of education and career, sexual desire and frustration, suffocation of a caged loveless marriage, numerous affairs, the futility of lust, the shame and sorrow of not finding love after repeated attempts, the loneliness and neurosis that stalks women especially and such other things which were not spoken of candidly are powerfully dealt with for the first time in her poetry.

Das has ventured into areas unclaimed by society and provided a point of reference for her colleagues. She has transcended the role of a poet and simply embraced the role of a very honest woman. The reader often feels that he is in the presence of a writer who is highly gifted and skilful, largely emotional and subjective, and who is ever celebrating the charms of the body and the hungers of the sex, without getting him bored even for a while. She redefines herself and liberates herself both as a woman and a poet. She struggles to cope with her problems and dilemmas.

Kamala Das, through all her poems, speaks against all kinds of dominance and oppression, and asserts the need of sanity in human relation which is the only mode of preservation of human existence on this planet.

In this paper I am going to deal with "Composition", "An Introduction", "The Freaks" and "The Looking Glass" to explain the mutilation and sufferings of women. Das's poetry reflects how women are caught within the web of expectations that is imposed on them by tradition and family.

Born in an erudite family in Kerela in 1934, the writings of Kamala Das were greatly influenced by her mother who was a renowned poetess in Malayalam and her uncle who was a great writer. Her love of poetry began at an early age through the influence of her mother and uncle.

Tradition is very strong in India and dictates many aspects of our lives. In India, regardless of religious differences, caste, class or regional location, tradition makes particular demands on the way women live their lives – from the clothes that they can wear, to their mobility, the kinds of jobs they take up and so. Psychologists have observed that as young girls grow into adolescence and womanhood, they comply more and more with the feminine roles demanded of them. Issues concerning women are the recurring themes in the volumes of Kamala Das. Women's social unrest in respect of education and career, sexual desire and frustration, suffocation of a caged loveless marriage, numerous affairs, the futility of lust, the shame and sorrow of not finding love after repeated attempts, the loneliness and neurosis that stalk women especially and such other things which were not spoken of candidly are powerfully dealt with for the first time in her poetry. She protests against the marginalisation of women and social injustices and communicates a powerful female sensibility in her poetry.

Kamala Das was married at the age of fifteen to a man who was much older and employed in a city. He came to be a father to his wife and his children. When Das wished to begin writing, her husband supported her decision to increase the family's income. Young Kamala, who harboured many romantic illusions, was not able to relate them to a husband, who seemed paternal, and schoolmasterish with a strong sense of do's and don'ts. This dissatisfaction is a dominant feature of her poems. However she was allowed to meet young men of her age and to develop her mental faculties and also her creative talents. She was allowed to do all these and more, but she was not allowed to forget her role as a wife, mother and housekeeper. In her poems, we see the young bride longing for freedom without knowing exactly what that freedom is and from whom. It may be assumed that Kamala resented her domestic duties when the creative urge came upon her and she had to suppress them for daily chores. She is the first Indian woman who openly talks about the sexual desires and experiences of Indian women. Her poems are known for their honest explorations of women's social unrest in respect of education and career, sexual desire and frustration, suffocation of a loveless marriage, urban life, women's roles in traditional Indian society, the political and personal struggles of marginalised people and such other things which were not spoken candidly earlier are powerfully dealt for the first time in her poems.

In December 1999, she converted to Islam and assumed the name of Kamala Suraiya. There are countless accounts about the life of Kamala Das. She always had media attention focused on her, because of bravado and eye-catching sound bites. We can say she was a forerunner to all the bold and beautiful women who were to come. She had zest and lust for life so essential for the mind of a poet.

Kamala Das is a tale weaver – weaving the rhythm of life into a tale of soul – a poet who loves to be loved in silence.

Man-woman Liaison in Kamala Das's Poems

Poetry springs from the angst in the soul, when all material comforts have been taken care of the thoughts of man turn towards her/his spiritual growth. Kamala Das opined, "A poet's raw material is not stone or clay, it is her personality." These lines tell us that theme of most poems are autobiographical. She traces an inward journey and adds words that stimulate and add weight to her poems. She is generally in a mood of confession. The reader gets the feeling that she is letting out personal secrets which she feels should not be kept under wraps. So, we see the secret thrill of a naughty child playing mind games with her readers, and also leaving them gasping for more.

When I was exposed to the writings of Kamala Das, I found that while the poetess spoke through her words, there were many implied meanings to the lines that she wrote. Her prime concern has been the age old relationship between man and woman. One is aware that right from Adam and Eve, man and woman have come together and lived together agreeing to disagree. This relationship has always been fraught with troubles. The cosmic cause of procreation is fulfilled by the tug-of-war and the attraction between opposites. This relationship has always been held up as one ordained by gods and therefore not to be questioned. However, Kamala Das questions this blind acceptance of matrimony and its inherent quality of subjugation of women and their bodies. Often in her poems, she shows up the unfairness of this union. In one of her poems she asks a question to all women: "woman is this happiness, this lying buried beneath a man?" Reading between these lines, we see a request to all women to rationalise the physical aspect of sexual union.

Kamala Das couches her dissatisfaction in plain words. Only a woman can understand the tragedy and torture that a woman endures in silence. The poetess is extra careful, not to offend her husband or any other man. Certain critics may call her a hypocrite given to verbal gimmicks. But, one feels that the depth of her poems have to be found by reading between the words, that is what this paper aims to explore. Her language is controlled, honest and free. But, very expressive of the angst felt by a woman trying to build a name in a man's world. The charge of being a nymphomaniac by critics also unsettles her sensitive mind. It is rather unfair too. It is so easy to label women who do not conform.

All Kamala Das's poems express her search for spirituality in the emotion called love. In her childish mind she idealised love, but physical encounter with this emotion left her feeling empty and cheated. So, she sets out to verbalise her discontent. Coming as she did from the milieu of the middle class Indian woman, she did not openly defy the norms of matrimony, but she expressed a desire to do so in her poems. Only a reader capable of reading between the lines can see and understand the deep agony of a woman forced to succumb to an insensitive man.

Frustration and Identity Crisis in Kamala Das's Poems

Women are more prone to identity crisis and frustration than men. Literary writings on women, for women and of women, many times incite a rebellion against the patriarchal norms of society. They draw distinct lines among the main elements that go into the composition of a feminist psyche and identity. They lay bare the accepted myths of male superiority; celebrate the sensuous and sexual reality of women. Often women rise from the embers of tragedy to make a name and niche for themselves. These characters become models for social change and attitudes. But in literature of different lands and from varied cultures, we still find the poignant lone women searching for answers and finding their true identities and the reason for their suffering and frustration. There is crisis in understanding of these identities. They are unaware of their status, and what their actual roles are. Are they mere wives, teachers, mothers, etc? They are always confused seeking their true identities. Their troubles differ only in degrees from others of their kind across the globe.

The two women poets Sylvia Plath and Kamala Das who come from vastly different countries, are remarkably close in their confessional mode of poetic expression, in which they speak of their problems and identity crisis. Both the poets vocalise their resistance to tradition, based on male domination or conventions.

Kamala Das is known for honesty and exploration of hidden emotions of a female mind at an international level through her confessional writings. Though her poems, no doubt, are about love and sex and so very interesting, they also bear a note of frustration and identity crisis. She speaks out her heart based on her own premises. She redefines herself and liberates herself both as a woman and a poet. She struggles to cope with her problems and dilemmas. She does not attempt to intellectualise nor does she attempts to spiritualise. She makes a discovery of human existence and narrates her experiences vividly and passionately. She rejects masks and roles and refuses to accept the limitations of her biology. She feels exploited and cheated by the civilisation of which she is a part. She seems to find no way out of her tormented inner world and knows that there can be no easy solutions. Analyses of her poems reveal that she presents her 'own mutilated self,' tormented by both past and present, and lost in deep sense of crisis.

This paper doesn't attempt a general appreciation of her poetic appreciation, but restricts itself to examining the desperation that colours a single, fairly typical poem, "Composition", which appeared in 1973 in the volume titled *The Old Playhouse and Other Poems*. This interpretation is based on psychoanalytical theory of signification. "Composition" embraces diverse moods as passionate attachment, agonising gilt, nauseating disgust and inhuman bitterness.

The poem has different stanzas of varying length. In the first stanza, the speaker says that she faces the sea, heard long ago as a ceaseless whisper in a shell; thereafter heard at night as breaking surf while she lay beside her grandmother. The house has since crumbled and the old woman is dead. The second stanza speaks of the loss of innocence, the tragedy of growth, the discovery of horror, the speaker's removal from the sea, and the sea's recurrence in her dreams. The third unit tells of marriage, and sexual interactions with both men and women, none of which appease, and most of which require play-acting. It ends with the speaker saying that she misses her grandmother. The fourth stanza reiterates the futility and sameness of all sexual encounters, and the indifference of the external world to the soul. The fifth stanza recalls the time when the speaker's grandmother invited her to spend a night in the old family home and waited for her with a lit lamp, but the speaker did not/ could not go. The sixth stanza presents the tawdry, jumbled world of prostitution, marriage, friendship, and enmity. Nothing is better or more than anything else. It closes with a call of despair and a longing for a walk into the sea for rest. The seventh and final stanza declares this to be impossible. Even the crumbling of the self brings no rest; the pains continue; the cells cannot escape; immortality of the consciousness is a certainty. The only freedom is the freedom to 'discompose', a word that acquires weight in the light of the poem's title "Composition".

The poem "Composition" is about love and is pessimistic in tone. Her personal frustrations and sense of loneliness add a note of intensity to the poem. The poetess remembers how she could hear the sound of the sea when she lived in the house of her grandmother. But soon her grandmother died. She looks into the minds of women and expresses their worlds for us. She says, "The tragedy of life is not death but growth, I was busy growing..." Growth is the real tragedy of life not death. The poetess grew and almost forgot the sea. Yet, she often dreamt of the sea waves. When she got married, her husband allowed her freedom to be. But she did not get love from anybody. Her husband did not love her and she missed her grandmother. She asked her husband, "am I hetero/am I lesbian/or am I just plain frigid?" These lines show that she lacks knowledge of her own self and there is crisis in her search for true identity. The poetess says that all women are physically alike; they only differ in the souls: "We are all alike, only the souls vary." She makes it clear that women are used as toys by men. "Deep, deep pain.../I have failed. /I feel my age and my uselessness. All I want now is to take a long walk into the sea and lie there resting." She sadly says that now she is no longer young and thus has become unappealing to her husband. This makes her feeling a deep pain in herself. We see this poem is about her suffering and frustration. The poem is reflective; a sense of hopelessness and aging is portrayed. A soul is dying from lack of spirit.

Kamala Das turned to writing in English after having written in Malayalam, her mother tongue. In "An Introduction" she writes:

> The language I speak
> Becomes mine, its distortations, its queerness
> All mine, mine alone. It is half English, half
> Indian, funny perhaps, but it is honest,
> It is as human as I am human...

"An Introduction" voices the poet's quest for identity and fulfilment. It is about pain and love. In "An Introduction" we see rebellion or protest against domination of the world by males, it is one of the recurring themes in this poem. Furthermore, we have here a poem of revolt against conventional thought and against the restraints which society imposes upon women. Kamala Das's feminism or her advocacy of the rights of women clearly appears here. It focuses on pertaining questions relating to womans identity. In "An Introduction", Das universalises and makes public traditionally private experiences, suggesting that women's personal feelings of longing and loss are part of the collective experience of womanhood.

> I am saint. I am the beloved and the
> Betrayed. I have no joys which are not yours, no
> Aches which are not yours. I too call myself I.

"An Introduction", a poem included in Kamala Das's first volume of poetry, *Summer in Calcutta (1965)*, begins with a statement that shows her frank distaste for politics, especially in politically free India ruled by a chosen elite. The poet asserts her right to speak three languages, and defends her choice to write in two—her mother-tongue, Malayalam, and English. She doesn't like to be advised in this matter by any guardian or relations. Her choice is her own: authentic and born of passion. The poet looks upon her decision to write in English as natural and humane.

From the issue of the politics of language the poem then passes on to the subject of sexual politics in a patriarchy-dominated society where a girl attaining puberty is told about her biological changes by some domineering parental figure. As the girl seeks fulfilment of her adolescent passion, a young lover is forced upon her to traumatise and coerce the female-body since the same is the site for patriarchy to display its power and authority. When thereafter, she opts for male clothing to hide her femininity, the guardians enforce typical female attire, with warnings to fit into the socially determined attributes of a woman, to become a wife and a mother and get confined to the domestic routine. She is threatened to remain within the four walls of her female space lest she should make herself a psychic or a maniac. But the poet is an individual woman trying to voice a universal womanhood and trying to share her experiences, good or bad, with all other women. Love and sexuality are a strong component in her search for female identity and the identity consists of polarities. The poem ends with repetitions of 'I' to suggest vindication of the body and the self.

In "An Introduction", Das criticises the institution of marriage which gives a man a legal right to commit marital rape on his teenage bride. She refuses to fit in the constructed role of "a girl", "a wife". She refuses to be weak and passive and self-less, self-denying, sacrificing and compliant angel under a masculine value system. The society demanded only one thing from her which she could not accept. It was "Fit in oh, /Belong, cried the categorisers". This individually alienation only increased her frustration. It finds expression in many things like her obsession with death and many imagined or real extra-marital relationships. Every thought and impulse keeps claiming its own identity from her.

In "The Freaks", Kamala Das releases an important aspect of a woman's psychology of love in her refusal to be pinned down to passive man. In "The Freaks", she analyses unfulfilled love. She identifies the lovers as her husband and herself and calls them freaks. The poem unravels the chasm between desire and its fulfillment.

In "The Freaks", Das says: "who can help us who have lived so long and have failed in love". The concluding section of the poem brings to the surface the problematic of a woman's identity, the male identity is everywhere taken for granted as suggested by the image 'the sword in the sheath'. The poem ends with the enumeration of unconventional roles a woman is not expected to play by categorisers. But not withstanding moral–socio–political categorisation, every woman has a self and the subjective need to call herself 'I'. In this poem the quest for identity of a woman as a woman goes a long way in making the self out of various disjunctive psychosomatic pressures which make her sometimes a victim and sometimes a crazy woman in whom we find an evaluating reason. Her experience of isolation, instead of being internalised surfaces and becomes part of a woman's experience in its macro–cosmic implication in the concluding lines of this poem.

In "The Freaks", Das describes male body as a source of corruption and exploitation and the female body as storehouse of beauty and chastity misused to the maximum. Evidently the poetess has drawn an ugly picture of the love–lorn man, who has 'a sun–stained cheek', 'a dark cavern in mouth', and 'uneven teeth' protruding forward. These lines evoke the image of saturation in sex–act, but all the same highlights her sense of bitterness in his contact.

"The Freaks" must be viewed in the light of Das's feminine consciousness. She acquired this consciousness under hostile circumstances dependent upon the society of her childhood days. Repressive attributes caused fragmentation to herself. As a poet, she is conscious of her creative faculties and tries to break chains and restraints. She indulges in selfawareness, selfexposure and selfintrospection in order to define herself poetically. The aim of the poet is not selfexposure, but selfdiscovery and selfexamination. Das structures selfexploration in order to search her lost identity as a woman and as a poet. In the crowded world of men and women, she finds herself utterly alone and describes an ache growing inside her and disturbing her. She examines her private life because that is the authentic life for her.

The poem "The Looking-Glass" suggests that women are the untouchables of love, in that the very things society labels dirty are the things the women are supposed to give. The poem implies that a restrained love seems to be no love at all; only a total immersion in love can do justice to this experience.

In the poem "The Looking Glass" frustration and hope go side by side. She gives certain guidelines as how to please and entertain the man. Then all of a sudden frustration comes to her. She becomes pessimistic. She has fears and doubts about losing her dear man. She says: "Oh yes, getting a man to love is easy, but living without him afterwards may have to be faced. A living without life when you move around, meeting strangers, with your eyes that gave up their search, with ears that hear only his last voice calling out your name and your body which once under his touch had gleamed like burnished brass, now drab and destitute."

At the outset, in "The Looking Glass", Das outlines to women how they should behave during sexual contact with a man. After giving some advice she warns about the real difficulty a woman faces. It is that this particular lover, with whom she has had the most pleasurable experiences of the sexual act, will leave her, never to come back. She would be unable to find a substitute for him and her life would become meaningless to her. Her eyes would keep searching for somebody like the departed lover, but she would not find anyone just like him. This predicament would lead her into a state of total despair and frustration. To live without her lover makes her life a living without life. It is the tragedy for a woman that she does not get emotional involvement from her man. The man enjoys her body but for the woman, it becomes life long suffering. In absence of her lover, her body, which was once very attractive, would then lose its charm and would become unexciting. Much of the ideas expressed may not have been experienced but they have been much brooded over, on the anvil of the mind.

Thus "The Looking Glass" brings out the fate of women in a male dominated society. They must accept their role as a sex toy passively. This makes their life frustrating. Though the poetess advises women about what they should do to win their lover, yet the sense of loss and bitter despair lingers. She is confused and does not know what her actual role is and faces loss of identity. She is unaware whether being with a man, who only gives her physical love, makes her happy or unhappy? But towards the end of the poem, she speaks of the frustration and suffering that women face.

Coupled with her exploration of women's needs is an attention to eroticism. The longing to lose one's self in passionate love is discussed in "The Looking Glass" from *The Descendants*. The narrator of the poem urges women to give their man "what makes you women". The things which society suggests are dirty or taboo are the very things which the women are supposed to give. The "musk of sweat between breasts, the warm shock of menstrual blood" should not be hidden from one's beloved. In the narrator's eyes, love should be defined by this type of unconditional honesty. A woman should "Stand nude before the glass with him," and allow her lover to see her exactly as she is. Likewise, the woman should appreciate even the "fond details" of her lover. Even if the woman may have to live "Without him" someday, the narrator does not seem to favor bridling one's passions to protect one's self. A restrained love seems to be no love at all; only a total immersion in love can do justice to this experience. Much like the creators of ancient Tantric art, Das makes no attempt to hide the sensuality of the human form; her work seems to celebrate its joyous potential while acknowledging its concurrent dangers.

Critical Reception

Critical response to Das's poetry has been intimately connected to critical perception of her personality and politics; her provocative poetry has seldom produced lukewarm reactions. While reviewers of Das's early poetry have praised its fierce originality, bold images, exploration of female sexuality, and intensely personal voice, they lamented that it lacked attention to structure and craftsmanship. Some scholars have found powerful feminist images in Das's poetry, focusing on critiques of marriage, motherhood, women's relationships to their bodies and power over their sexuality, and the roles women are offered in traditional Indian society. Many critics have analysed Das as a "confessional" poet, writing in the tradition of Sylvia Plath, Anne Sexton and Denise Levertov. Some scholars have deemed Das's poetry, autobiography, and essays frustratingly inconsistent, self-indulgent, and equivocal, although they, too, have praised her compelling images and original voice. Such commentators have suggested that she is both overexposed and overrated. Other scholars have connected the emphasis on the self in Das's work to larger historical and cultural contexts and complicated, shifting postcolonial identities. Indian critics have disagreed about the significance of Das's choice to write of her experiences as an Indian woman in English; some scholars suggest that, in her shunning of traditional aesthetic form, she has created a new language for the expression of colonial contradictions. Despite disagreement over the aesthetic qualities and consistency of her body of poetry, scholars agree that she is an important figure whose bold and honest voice has re-energised Indian writing in English.

Conclusion

The tragedy of Kamala Das is not so much because of her situation, but her rationalisation of every experience. The protection and possessiveness of the husband only fuelled her sense of alienation and frustration. We see two individuals bound by marriage living on different planes-one earthy and physical, the other dreamy and spiritual. Never the twain could meet or communicate. The tragic feature to receive spiritually sexual satiation leads her to seek it elsewhere. Each new relationship reinforced the vacuum and intensified her disappointment. Her experience led her to write about isolation, turbulence and depression. But the poetess is an individual woman trying to voice the universal lament of womanhood and trying to share her good and bad experiences, with all other women. Love and sexuality are strong components in her search for her female identity; this identity is made up of polarities. The world of Kamala Das is exclusively concerned with the personal experience of love expressed in poetry. For her ideal love is the satiation of both body and soul. It is the experience of going beyond sex through sex.

Kamala Das analyses man-woman relationship from an anti-romantic angle and protest against womanhood suppressed by ethics and taboos. Mrs. Das, who received no formal education, no pompous university degree, stands on her own merit and is placed on the pinnacle of reputation and distinction among Indo-English poets of today. Her scintillating verse has that irresistible force and tilting rhythm in it which captures the readers attention immediately. The poetess admirably comes through the dictum of William Wordsworth when he pronounced that "poetry is the spontaneous overflow of powerful feelings".

Thus through the poems "Composition", "An Introduction", "The Freaks" and "The Looking Glass", I have explained the mutilation and sufferings of women by Kamala Das.

Works Cited

Alladi Uma, *Kamala Das: Critical Essay,* (MLA), 2003.

— "What's in a Genre?: Kamala Das's My Story" *Literary Criterion* 32, no. 3 (1996): 69-75.

Blackmur R.P., *Language as a Gesture,* London, 1954, p. 269.

Das Kamala, *My Story,* New Delhi, 1976.

— "Sex, Mindless surrender or Humming Fiesta", *Femina,* June 6, 1975.

— Obscenity in Literature and Arts, ed. Suresh Kohli, New Delhi, 1973.

Das N.D.R.Chandra Nigamananda, *Ecology. Myth. and Mystery,* 2007.

Dwivedi, A.N. *Indo-Anglian Poetry,* Allahabad, Kitab Mahal, 1979.

— *Kamala Das & Her Poetry,* Eastern Book Cooperation, 2006.

Eliot T.S., "Tradition and Individual Talent", *Selected Essays,* London, McMill, p. 21.

Iqbal Kaur, *Perspective on Kamala Das' Poetry,* 1995.

Iyengar K.R.S., *Indian Writing in English,* Bombay, 1973, p.680.

King Bruce, *Modern Indian Poetry in English,* 1987.

Kohli Suresh, "The Poetic Craft of Kamala Das", *Thought,* Vol.XX, No.2, March 16, 1968, p.17.

Kundu Rama, *Indian Writing in English,* New Delhi, Atlantic, 2003.

Mishra, Shashi Bhushan, Autobiography in Indian Writing in English, Delhi, Adhyayan, 2004, vii, p. 103.

Nabar Vrinda, *Endless Female Hungers: Study of Kamala Das,* 1994.

Paranjape Makarand, *Indian Poetry in English,* 1993.

Peeradina Saleem, *Contemporary Indian Poetry in English,* 1972.

Prasad Hari Mohan and Chkradhar Prasad Singh, *Indian Poetry in English,* 1985.

Rahman Anisur, *Expressive form in the poetry of Kamala Das,* September, 1981.

Raveendran N.V., *Aesthetics Of Sensuality A Stylistic Study Of The Peotry Of Kamala Das,* Atlantic Publishers & Distributors, 2000.

Surendran K.V., *Indian English Poetry,* 2002.

6

Polarities of Existence: Body as Text in Kamala Das's *My Story*

— *Prajna Paramita Panigrahi*

> If woman lived in a different country from the men and never had read any of their writings, they would have a literature of their own and a different image about themselves, for who can understand a woman better than a woman herself.
>
> —(J.S. Mill on "The Subjection of Women", 1969)

The Indian novel in English was the product of a demand for socio-political reforms, the revival of past traditions, the search for a national identity and the increasing awareness of the role of individual in society. Set against the backdrop of colonial India, the novel fascinated the common man with the novelty of its exotic form and its capability of representing a changing world in its various dimensions. This new genre of literature, notwithstanding its versatility, still positioned men at the centre of the narrative, and a woman's story, even if presented by a woman, was from a male perspective. Her portrayal of character would either be hyperbolic or marginalised.

Male writers seem to be handicapped in painting her in her true colours. The inner conflict of a suffering woman and her ability to protest the patriarchal order are very rarely explored. As public events assumed greater importance than that which happened in the privacy of the homes; 'woman' with a separate entity, failed to impress the novelist. She was "romantic, charming, graceful, cultured, wise, courageous ... such stuff as dreams were made on" (Jain, 36). Obedience and faithfulness perfected her. She accepted the stereotyped roles assigned to her by tradition.

Literature being the reflection of the real world shows the image of woman as a necessary construct of the consciousness and milieu of the literary artist. Patriarchal society condemned female writing and as a result, authorship assumed the prerogative of the male sex. Femininity or treatment of the female self, strictly adhered to the male's definition and creative ability. As the control of the text rests on the writer, the image evolves moves and develops along the schema of the artist. The image, itself, has little scope for change or challenges the dictum. Passive or aggressive, the *Angel* or the *Monster*, the woman is reduced to a stereotype. Conformity is thus, an oft-trodden path for the woman-subject in the male writings. On the other hand, the women writer struggles to establish her own precursor in order to overcome these established icons. Deviating from structured models, they seek to find a literature of their own; a hidden talent to mirror their quest for 'self-definition'.

The interaction of her biological constitution and her social environment forms the basic nature of a woman. Her experiences and emotions are hereby related to her perceptions of the inside/outside world. A woman's writing, too, is a reflection of such processes entwined in social, economic and political corrosions. Simone de Beauvoir's classic statement, "One is not born, but rather becomes a woman", suggests that female identity is constructed on the basis of her sexuality. In her biological difference to man, her body is the site for gender-bias, exploitation, violence and abuse. It is also the ground to analyse relationship, outgrow emotions, balance perceptives and offer cognitive analysis for self-identity. Meenakshi Thapan defines:

> ... a woman experiences her body, sexuality and feminine identity as a social being located in a particular cultural setting with its dominant values and norms. (5)

Recent feminist theories argue that traditional scholarship views woman as the biological body, capable of reproduction, nurturance and recreation. It does not attach any due importance to the feminine mind which is equally capable of independent rationalisation and objective outlook. Such a view results in polarities and attempts to structure dualities like male/ female, culture/ nature, objective/ subjective, order/ disorder, reason/ emotion, etc. The feminine self is attributed to the subordinate position, a disarray of ideas and emotions trapped in a socially constructed body.

Not so neatly defined as her Western counterpart, the feminine image in India is ambivalent. Tradition locates her persona as both an epitome of devotion and sacrifice and an evil power capable of destruction; hence the need for a regulation of her sexuality increases. The female body is controlled through various socio-political measures, allowing little or no space for her expression of identity. Chastity, virtue and purity are extolled as great feminine virtues and also symbols of family's honour and the community at large.

A woman's experience of her body is largely that of shame (*lajja*) as she is seen as transgressing family and social moral normal in one way or another. The moral domain for woman is therefore always defined and policed by the other. In a sense, woman's body is often no longer *her* body but has been taken over by the community of both men and women, to establish and legitimise its image in society. (Thapan 6)

A matrix of Indian women writers, of the present era, provides a wide spectrum of varied experiences of women along with a direct and subjective analysis of her sexuality, her risk and joy at childbirth and her painful segregation from the male-dominated society. Novels, under such implications, stress the gap between the male and the female subconscious and a reconstruction of female experience. Opting for a redefinition of history, Coppelia Kahn implies:

> History has been a record of male experience, written by men from a male perspective. What has been denigrated historically significant has been deemed so according to a valuation of power and activity in a public world.... It is therefore imperative for historians of women to reconstruct the female experience and to full the blank pages and make the silences speak.
>
> (qtd. in Sumita Parmar, Singh 232-233)

As a revolt against the undermining of femininity, fiction by women writers does not encounter poverty, deprivation or economic and domestic upheavals. It mirrors the fierce struggle for a woman's survival amidst prejudice, violence and violation of her body and mind in a high-class, city-bred life. It exposes the adverse value system which affronts the female psyche at every phase. Since human experiences are not fixed or individualistic, but a series of social procedures, woman too experiences the same phenomenon. Varied and disjointed, female experiences, as delineated by women writers are more intimate, personal and subjective. Her location in different settings such as the community, the family, the workplace, etc. shapes her individual mind.

Intrinsically a poet and a reputed columnist Kamala Das, seeks to break down barriers of a patriarchal society. Brought up in the last phases of British rule in India, she is caught in the turmoil of a placidity and creation. The new world is yet to be formed, and the old world was passing by. Her poems reflect her conflict and more so, her need to break free from the conventions that hold her down. "I began to write poetry with the ignoble aim of wooing a man. There is lot of love in my poems."(Nabar 19). Her awareness of her body is can be seen as being constitutive of her Self. It relates to her self-identity. The body has a symbolic and cultural value and is either shaped, defined or constrained by societal norms. It is often the site for violence, exclusion and abuse.

Helen Cixous views that, till date, women's writing has been directly or indirectly controlled by a masculine economy. In order to justify her own creative self, woman must be initiated to express her deeply-felt emotions. She highlights:

> ... woman must write herself: must write about women and bring women to writing, from which they have been driven away as violently as from their bodies.... Woman must put herself into the text – as into the world and into history – by her own movement.
>
> (qtd. in Vidhu Vema, 278)

Kamala Das sketched the confrontation of desires with feminine modesty. The stereotypical image of the woman is conditioned to believe that woman needs to sublimate her sexuality in order to achieve that innate goodness. Thus, Indian woman is schooled to suppress her natural instincts. Das writes:

> Dress in sarees, be girl.
> Be wife, they said. Be embroiderer, be cook.,
> Be a quarreller with servants....("Introduction")

She is the "angel in the house", beautiful, charming, obedient, and unselfish. Virtuous and culturally sound, the Indian woman in Das accepts the monotony of marriage and the myriad promises that it holds. *My Story* can be considered to be a major attempt of a woman writer to discuss physical intimacy, which is still considered to be a taboo for many women writers. Das is caught in the emotional turmoil of confronting to norms and yet being true to her Self. Tradition prescribes a role which she cannot adjust. She becomes a wife, not knowing which category she belongs to.

> Was every married adult a clown in bed, a circus performer? I hate marriage...I hate to show myself naked to anyone. (*My Story* 70)

Her first experiences about her body begin with the attraction of a female friend. She describes the intimacy in an inhibited manner, which in turn justifies the growth of the female self. " Her fingers traced the outlines of my mouth with a gentleness that I had never dreamt of finding. She kissed my lips" (*My Story* 79). She confesses that she was half in love with her. Notwithstanding the traditional makeup of her mind, her body is aware of the first onslaughts of sexuality. She finds the human body enigmatic, yet surprising. On the other hand, her husband shocks her, on the first night of her marriage:

> Then without warning he fell on me, surprising me by the extreme brutality of the attack (*My Story* 89).

Das's husband termed her as "frigid", while marital rape had numbed her. A woman is nurtured and understood essentially by her sexuality and her reproductive value.

But,
I must pose,
I must pretend,
I must act the role
Of happy woman,
Happy wife.
I must keep the right distance
Between me and the high.
I must keep the right distance
Between me and the low. ("The Suicide")

Many decades later, Deshpande gives a vivid picture of a married pair, where sexual intimacy is a wordless routine. In *That Long Silence* Jaya seethes in anger and frustration:

> I could time it, almost to the second, the whole process of our love-making, from the first devious wooing to the moment he turned away from me offering me his hunched back. (85)

Descriptions of physical intimacy in women writers posits woman at the receiving end of sordidness and humiliation. Brought up in an authoritarian atmosphere where her father's word was law and her mother had little say even in household matters, Kamala looked forward to an understanding and loving husband. His attitude to sex, aggressive and brutal made her complacent and immune to his so-called acts of love. His flirtatious relations with his cousins made Kamala indignant:

> I made up my mind to be unfaithful to him, at least physically. (*My Story* 95)

Kamala Das has explored man-woman relationship in bold and concrete terms and paved way for writers like Shobha De, who conveys that female sexuality can be a liberating and empowering force for women. Anuradha Roy comments:

> These writers have contributed substantially to the mammoth task of demystifying women and have helped to construct the individuality of women even in its physical and sexual dimensions. They have refused to be silenced on

> issues of sexual morality and ruthlessly exposed the shameful duplicity of standards. (49)

Women, trapped in boredom and restraint, move out to indulge in sensual pleasures. Sex and love is a game, with a changing partner to keep the novelty of life. Her fiction encompasses the psycho-sexual accomplishments of the female. Termed as "vertical movement" or "voyage within", the inner workings of the mind are aptly dealt with. Replete with sexual encounters and physical intimacy, Das analyses the deep urges of the human soul, craving for Truth and Perfection.

She projected their intimate experiences, sexual and moral dilemmas. Simone de Beauvoir rightly observes:

> The women of today are in a fair way to dethrone the myth of femininity; they are beginning to affirm their independence in concrete ways, but they do not succeed in living completely the life of a human being. (30)

Women are socially and culturally tuned to "fit in" and adjust to tradition and practice. Hence, they organise themselves as the sole torch bearers of familial and social honour. Kamala crossed all limits of a married woman, basking in infidelity. She justifies, "I was ready for love....Ripe for a sexual banquet" (*My Story* 95). Crossing the threshold, she moved to embrace her many lovers. From a handsome bricklayer across the street to a vivid pen friend across the country, she offered her body to their satisfaction. She enjoyed her newly found freedom. Her body was a gift for anyone. Irrespective of her lovers and their charms, Kamala is an honest mother, who loves her sons and to some extent, respects her husband. " I let him take my body every night, hoping that the act would relax his nerves and make him tranquil." (*My Story* 102)

Discarding the cardinal principles of fidelity, faith and understanding in the institution of marriage, Das hints that submergence of male ego, through feminine tactics and sexual gratification can pave the way for female independence. Toril Moi, examining the sexually coloured texts of women writers in *Sexual/ Textual Politics* hints:

> I would like to believe in the multiplicity of sexually marked voices. I would like to believe in the masses, this indeterminable number of blended voices, this mobile of non-identified sexual marks whose choreography can carry, divide, multiply the body of each 'individual' whether he be classified as 'man' or 'woman' according to the criteria of usage. (173)

She struggles for survival and is brave enough to deal with the blows of Fate. Frustration creeps in many forms, but she is still proud to have her power intact. Her body is her source of strength and fulfillment. As her admirers multiplied, Das was blissfully happy. " I was like a poor girl who found herself rich all of a sudden."(*My Story* 145)

Exploring an individual's predicament in the myriad conversions of history and politics, the male writers of the new generation have treated women as a means to an end. She enhances recreates and rebuilds the stature of the protagonist (preferably male) rather than becoming a protagonist herself. Her presence adds a dimension to fiction that had hitherto been lacking. The female is thus, a supplement, a sexual object or an embodiment of destruction.

> Woman is allowed little or no space for an independent, self-perceived articulation, definition or expression of her sexuality. Her body becomes an instrument and a symbol for the community's expression of caste, class and communal honour. Chastity, virtue and above all, purity are extolled as great feminine virtues embodying the honour of the family, community and nation.
>
> (Thapan 6)

Das subverts the male ego. For her, it is the female ego which rushes out to welcome the male and savour its sexuality. It is the strength, the power to sublimate her desires, through this vocation and her body is the medium. She is candid enough to hint that old age has no respite for women:

> Was it no longer possible to lure a charming male into a complicated and satisfying love affair with the right words, right glances, the right gestures? Was I finished as a charmer? (*My Story* 145)

She is then entangled with an elderly man, known for his lustful ways, and it is in the autumn of her life that she finds ultimate satisfaction. She felt most secured in his arms, wishing to " grow in him like cancer" *(My Story,* 184). Her search was complete. She had reached the end of her destination. Fulfilled and joyous, her carnal desires died a natural death. She records:

> If my desires were lotuses in a pond, closing their petals at dusk and opening out at dawn once upon a time, they were totally dead, rotted and dissolved and for them there was no more to be a respouting. The pond had cleared itself of all growth. It was placid. (*My Story,* 209).

My Story is an honest appraisal of female sexuality and her need for sexual freedom. Her quest for identity leads her through many unequal relationships, each hurting her emotionally. Sexual exploits represents her attempts to be submerged to the other self, so much so that she loses a part of herself in every encounter. Rama Rani Lall, confirms:

> In *My Story* she attempts to define her identity as a woman and to create a space within her and around her in order to assert the legitimacy of her dreams and fantasies, and to express her hopes and frustrations. (Jain 233)

In a culturally-dominant society, the female self is often the victim of prejudices and convention. Harmony of individual aspirations and societal expectations is enforced submissiveness of the female sex. She journeys through the emotional upheavals to search her identity and ends up with the debarring of any male entity, in the process of self-realisation. She is conscious of her rights and is able to carve out a space for herself. Patriarchal forms of oppression teach her to develop her course of action, with a singleminded devotion. There is no looking back.

Women writers focus on the conflicts in man-woman relationship and the female psyche conditioning itself to survive the oppressive forces. The postIndependence Indian woman is aware of her rights, virtues, duties and also of convention. She has complete knowledge of her heritage and is proud to be part of the great tradition. Social obligations and moral responsibilities have conditioned her. She is also aware of her fears, weaknesses and limitations; the length of the road she can tread upon, the dangers she has to overcome. Her awareness of her Self has come full circle. But she has complete control over both her body and her mind; and is quite capable of maintaining a rightful balance between the two.

The female writers of the new generation stress on her adaptability and adjustments. She can be aptly compared to life's necessity, the water; taking the form and shape of any vessel she is poured into. She mingles into any surroundings and blossoms amidst any atrocious difficulties, thus smoothing the path for others to follow. She is the essence of the life force, the negation of which leads to a negation of life itself.

Works Cited

De Beauvoir, Simone. *The Second Sex*. 1949. Ed. and trans. H.M. Parshley, 1953, Harmondsworth, Penguin, 1974.

Deshpande, Shashi *That Long Silence*, New Delhi, Penguin, 1989.

Mill, J.S. qtd in. Jasbir Jain, Ed. *Women's Writing: Text and Context*, Jaipur, Rawat Publications, 1999.

Moi, Toril.

Nabar, Vrinda, *The Endless Female Hungers: A Study of Kamala Das*, New Delhi, Sterling Publishers Private Limited, 1994.

Roy, Anuradha, *Patterns of Feminist Consciousness in India Women Writers*, New Delhi, Prestige, 1999.

Thapan, Meenakshi, *Embodiment and Other Essays*, New Delhi, Oxford University Press, 1997.

7

Two Faces of Janus: Religious Motifs in the Poetry of Kamala Das

— *Purnendu Chatterjee*

> Real religion can exist ... not without a distinction between the spiritual and the profane... Religion is not so much a revelation to be attained by us in faith as *an effort to unveil the deepest layers of man's being and get into enduring contact with them.*[1] (italics mine)

Religion, thus, in its essence is a means of self-realisation. It does not reside in temples, mosques, churches or gurudwaras, but in the soul of human beings. Religious consciousness lies not in performing numerous rituals and going on pilgrimages but in being able to go beyond the limitations of flesh and blood to an understanding of the soul and in being able to distinguish between the "spiritual"—not the sacred—and the "profane", not the unholy. It is this universal concept of religion that underlies the poetic oeuvre of Kamala Das. In *Annamalai Poems* (VIII), the poet acknowledges the difficulty of the task:

> ...Other
> journeys are all so easy but
> not the inward one, the longest
> route home and the steepest
> descent...[2]

The "inward" journey is the effort to go deep into the soul in the process of self-realisation. The "journey" is difficult because it involves the shedding of the ego, severance of material and earthly associations and a complete merger of the mind and the soul. Das is too honest to deny the domain of the body and roam in the vague regions of metaphysics. The body is as true as the soul and in order to reach the soul, one must go through the body. Das is covertly positing the universal concept that physical energies must be transformed into spiritual energy in the course of the "inward" journey.

Kamala Das was born in a Nair (Namboodri Brahmin) family of Malabar. She embraced Islam in 1999 at the age of 65 and assumed the name Kamala Suraiya. This essay seeks to explore the inflections of Hinduism and Islam on the poetry of Kamala Das. In doing so, the essay will highlight that Das uses the Hindu myth of Radha-Krishna and the Islamic concept of Allah not as religious concepts, but as literary and existential motifs and metaphors. In her poetry, she attempted to humanise and idealise Krishna and Allah. In her treatment of the Radha-Krishna myth, she follows the strategy of the Varkari poet, Janabai. Just as Janabai humanised Lord Vithoba, Kamala Das humanised Lord Krishna. In her treatment of Islam, she is akin to the Sufi sect. Moreover, her melioristic vision that is reflected in her love for humanity lends a religious overtone to her poetry.

Before, I move on, I wish to pause for an instant and clarify a point. This critical essay might run the risk of falling into the domain of what Wimsatt and Beardsley calls "the intentional fallacy". However, what gives me courage and conviction to move on with this humble effort is the fact that in the present context, it may be safely asserted that Das's "intending or meaning mind" and her "effective intention or operative mind"[3] do not differ, but overlaps symmetrically.

I

Das reflected an eclectic view towards Hinduism. The detailed rituals performed by her grandmother come under the scope of mild irony in the poem "Blood":

> She was really simple.
> Fed on God for years,
> All her feasts were monotonous
> For the only dish served was always God.

It is, indeed, difficult to miss the impact of the telling adjective "simple" as it is impossible to ignore the tedium involved in the meticulous practice of detailed rites. The critical manner in which Das regarded the rituals and observances, which have always for the Hindus remained at the core of their form of life, shows that she was a believer in *nirguna-Brahman,* the "distinctionless [sic] Reality". God is the one, unified force—the primal flood, the moving fount of Being, in Hindu mythopoeia, the Brahman,

> ... the undying reality
> which does not dissolve though all beings dissolve[4]

It is obvious then that Das does not look for Godhead in the figure of Lord Krishna. She rather sought for an ideal lover in the figure of Krishna. In fact, her search for an ideal lover is rooted in her deep sense of alienation. She languished in the folds of a matrilineal society that was quickly shifting its centre of gravity towards a male hegemonic society. A short passage marked with heavy sadness and little sarcasm from her brings out the pathetic predicament of women in the Nair community to which she belonged:

> They kept themselves to the zenana never once raising their voices to express any emotion. They may have become excellent nuns but in that rarifying process they lost their identities, turning vague and colourless. Even the diseases that finally carried them away were vague and colourless. A breathlessness followed by fatigue and death. An attack of indigestion. Quick departures that underplayed the tragedy of their lives.[5]

Confined within this constrictive social macrocosm, Das found little comfort in the microcosm of her home. Her father was the dominating male and her mother was an introvert, always busy with her poetic creations. The obvious result was that the child found herself hopelessly moored in the mire of a loveless family. Her marriage at the tender age of 15 to a man who displayed homosexual advances even proved worse. While she craved for the ennobling and pleasurable experience of love, the obnoxious and odious experience of lust was bestowed upon her in copious measures.

The covetous desire for the body and only the body was indescribably horrible to Kamala Das, for lust is like being "bitten by a Krait who fills/The bloodstream with its accursed essences" ('Gino'). The erotic images and the candid references to the female body that abound in Das's love poems which are, in fact, loveless—the "obtrusive breasts" ("The Wild Bougainvillea"), "flabby thighs" ("Death is so Mediocre"), "warm shock of menstrual blood" ("The Looking Glass"), and there are scores of them—are dual attempts on the part of the poet to write off the body and, at the same time, tweak the noses of the patriarchal gods for their sham dislike of the female flesh.

With the hope of finding soulful love receding almost in embarrassment and the mind being filled with "coiling snakes of silence" ("The Freaks"), the poet harks back to the Indian tradition of the Varkari poet Janabai who had demythicised Lord Vithoba as her helper. Das demythicises Lord Krishna, the eighth avatar of Vishnu, in order to find in him an Ideal lover in whom she hopes to merge. Das unequivocally clarifies her attitude to Krishna:

> But illogical that I am from birth onwards, I have always thought of Krishna as my mate. ....It was only by imagining that he was with me that I could lie beneath my husband to give him pleasure.[6]

The image of Krishna is more real than the figure of her husband and this primacy of the image over the body is reliant on the psychosomatic course behind idealisation. She imbues both Radha and Krishna with the qualities of common human beings. The gloss of divinity that enfolds the Radha-Krishna myth is shed in Das's poetry. As Fritz Blackwell puts it:

> ... her (Kamala Das) concern is literary and existential, not religious; she is using a religious concept for a literary motif and metaphor.[7]

The mythical lovers are humanised and their relationship is often described in erotic terms. This brings into her poetic context the *Abhisarika* and *Sahaja* tradition of Sanskrit poetry.

The bliss of the mythical relation is contrasted to the frustration of a mundane loveless relation and, Das employed her favourite poetic strategy of disparity. the eternal lover is contrasted to the earthly lover. In the poem "A Man is a Season", the poet puts forward a contrast between the two lovers: To teach me this you let me toss my youth like coins Into various hands, you let me mate with shadows, You let me sing in empty shrines, you let your wife Seek ecstasy in others' arms."

> A man is a season,
> You are eternity,

The "You" is the eternal, archetypal lover to whom the persona is married. But before she can dissolve into the eternal lover, she must shed her ego. So, it is the eternal lover who makes her "mate" with the earthly lovers. Once she is humbled, once the ego is squeezed out of the self, as it were; through a sieve, she can find eternal bliss in the arms of the archetypal lover.

Humbling of the soul, which denotes a transcendence of the self, is a prerequisite for the congress with eternity. Conquering the obstacles of the body, in spite of all the grueling experience that such an attempt entails, in order to reach the soul is expressed in the poem "Advice to Fellow-Swimmers":

> When you learn to swim
> do not enter a river that has no ocean
> to flow into, ...
> go swim in the great blue sea
> Where the first tide you meet is your body,
> that familiar pest,
> but if you learn to cross it
> you are safe, yes, beyond it you are safe,
> For, even sinking would make no difference then.....

The body is a "pest" because it is the source of all sufferings. But once, the barrier of the body is traversed, one may rest assured, feel "safe", that the "great blue sea", the eternal and the infinite, lies in the offing: "nadyah syandamanah samudre astam gacchanti nama-rupe vihaya".[8] The river symbolises the temporal, the sea the eternal. The river flowing into the sea is a symbolic representation of the immortal soul leaving its temporary earthly abode and merging into the infinite.

Once the union with the eternal lover is effected there is no need to look beyond. The poet contentedly declares, "Your body is my prison, Krishna". Everything, love, beauty and truth, congeal. Ideal love, as conceived by imagination, is found to be true. The thought lends a calmness to her mind and enables her to smile even at the prospect of her death, as she does in the poem "My Morning Tree":

> Morning tree, on your brown branch, one day, I shall see a
> sudden flower, and know at once
> That my death is just a flower.

The poet visualises her death as a "flower" which shows her untroubled acceptance of death. Kamala Das, despite her patent obsession with death, is not pessimistic in her attitude to it. She is, in fact, able to visualise in death the incredible potentialities of a creative force. In line with Whitman, Das suggests that Death is not a simple negation of life; it leads to the escalation of the soul where Death is dead and only life exists. In *Annamalai Poems* (III), she projects the growth of soul that looks beyond death to be crowned at infinity:

> If only the
> human eye could look beyond the
> chilling flesh ....
> ... where would
> death be then, that meaningless word
> when life is all that there is, that
> raging continuity that
> often the wise ones recognise as God?

To Das, the soul is that which is sinless in the sinful, it is the pure, the unsullied – the immortal love – in this filth and dirt of a mortal body with its crude passions. Death eats away the body, but in this way, the soul grows towards the infinite. This is the grand spiritual discourse: the ingenuity of Death and the resurgence of the soul divine in its love divine.

II

Das's eclectic views towards Hinduism, her bitter protests against the dominant male discourse and her candid references to the body that were inspired by her sociological ambience as well as by her desire to write off the body, brought the ire of the Hindus upon her. She felt suffocated within the labyrinth of the society. For a long time she had been a mentor to two Muslim students: Irshad Ahmed and Imtiaz Amed. Irshad Ahmed is now one of the best authorities on Das's poetry. It is obvious that in close contact with them, she felt an affinity towards Islam. However, her decision to embrace Islam was not whimsical. She points out that her love for Islam knows no bounds because it was after a prolonged study of world religions that she felt drawn to the simplicity and sublimity of the message of Islam. Her conscience impelled her that she must join a faith, which would give her a better understanding of the moral purpose behind thc creation of the Universe. Moreover, the *purdah* attracted her as a means of potential security.

At the age of 65, with a mellowed poetic vision, she reoriented her earlier strategy with regard to Krishna and did not try to find an ideal lover in Allah. She rather looked for Allah's "features" on her "beloved's mien". The word "features" is a metaphor for qualities and she sought for a lover who in his soulful devotion to Allah would partake some of Allah's qualities. In her treatment of Islam, Das again shows an eclectic attitude, which is akin to the Sufi sect. Sufism is a religion based on the truth of life. Sufism is a way to travel to the presence of the Divine force and fill oneself with inner beauty and compassion. It is a mystic tradition that consists of a varied range of ideas and practices that emphasize on the attainment of divine love and compassion of the heart. Das follows Sufism that announces the *sadhna* of love, which lets the head be guided by the heart, gets over the conceptual dilemma in the realisation of the non-duality of self and the Absolute without disturbing the valuable diversity of religious faiths. Therefore, it is quite natural for Das to feel that the identities of Krishna and Allah are not different. So, she can state, with her characteristic boldness and candour, "I'm converting Krishna into Allah and making him the Prophet after naming him Mohammed."[9] When the Hindu fundamentalists trenchantly criticised her statement, she candidly made her position clear:

> As far as I am concerned God is an abstract entity and anyone can call Him by any name he likes. My critics should note that I have not called God by any name in my writing. I have always referred to God as an Almighty Power.[10]

Similarly, Kabir did suggest the essential unity of God by pointing out that he was the son of Rama And Allah—a sentiment that was applauded by philosopher-writers as different as Rabindranath Tagore and Octavio Paz.

Das's attitude to Islam is also analogous to Mu'tazilah, those who called themselves *"ahl al-tawhid wa al-ad"*[11] (people of unity and justice). The poet does not believe in man-made religions. She has always deeply felt that the present form of religion has lost its need and it has become as dangerous as an expired drug. God lies beyond the practiced religions. In "Ya Allah!" Poem-2, she asserts:

> I am she
> Who mistrusts cults
> Believes that You are not
> Connected to any religion,
> Old or new
> I cannot fold
> My wayward limbs to crawl into
> Coffins of religion.[12]

This is Das's *raison d'etre*. God is not the part of any religion. Dogmatic and fanatic religious practice is a "coffin" because it shuts out the world of reality that is peopled with the weak and the suffering and blinds the eye of reason. Rightly did Pandit Nehru in *Discovery of India* comment that much blood has been shed in the name of religion than in the name of anything else. Das believes that "love...primarily a thing of the heart... is the only true religion because it precedes all conventional religions."[13] The "love" that Das speaks of here is not a physical, materialist, narrow and selfish obsession, but a grand melioristic passion that aims to cater to all the suffering humanity that includes the poor house-builders, the miserable life of the eunuchs, the pitiful victims of generation gap, the hapless mothers who have lost their sons in war and the victimised Tamils and Sikhs. This is exactly in line with the teachings of *The Holy Quran*:

> Stand out firmly for justice, as witnesses to Allah, even as against yourselves, or your parents, or your kin, and whether it be (against) rich or poor: for Allah can best protect both. Follow not the lusts (of your hearts), lest ye swerve, and if ye distort (justice), verily, Allah is well acquainted with all that ye do (4:135).[14]

The concept of "justice" refers to the universal ethical principles of the right and, obviously, it stands against all the corruptions and evils on the universal plane of humanity. All human beings, irrespective of religious and socio-economic hiatus, are under the purview of this "justice". Human beings must avoid "lusts", for it blinds the eye of humanity and make people selfish, resulting in a distortion of "justice". This edification of *The Holy Quran* echoes the leitmotif of Das's melioristic vision. It is pertinent to point out that Das does not accept the teachings of *The Holy Quran* from the stance of a fanatic Muslim. For instance, she does not agree with the view that "Truly the Pagans are unclean; so let them not, after this year of theirs, approach the Sacred Mosque" (9:28).[15] This eclectic attitude of the poet has been the cause of much chagrin among the Muslim fundamentalists.

Das did not find the much coveted peace within the folds of Islam. The terrorist attacks of different Muslim factions, the destruction of the Buddhist idols at Bamian, the terrible atrocities of different terrorist groups, the excesses of nationalism, the religious intolerances and the cruelty meted out to humanity at large deeply shocked the sensibility of the poet. Reports of executions, random shootings, rapes and other atrocities were shocking to the poet. Her deep disillusion finds expression in an interview:

> God has no connection with any religion. There is no respect for women anywhere. Women are just an object of sensual pleasure.....You begin to seek spiritual freedom after the end of the menstrual cycle as I was, but there was none. I give no importance to religion now. God has been appropriated by a few people for their own selfish ends.[16]

III

Etymologically, the English word *religion* has been in use since the

13th century, loaned from *Anglo-French religiun* (11th century), ultimately from the *Latin religio*, "reverence for God or the gods, careful pondering of divine things, *piety*, the *res divinae*." The ultimate origins of Latin *religio* are obscure. It is usually accepted to derive from *ligare* 'bind, connect'; probably from a prefixed *re-ligare*, i.e. *re* (again) + *ligare* or 'to reconnect.' This interpretation is favoured by modern scholars such as Tom Harpur and Joseph Campbell, but was made prominent by St. Augustine, following the interpretation of Lactantius. Thus, religion in its purest essence has double implications: it pertains to human good as well as it furnishes to the needs of the soul.

Das conflates both the strains of religion in her poetic oeuvre. Vincent O' Sullivan aptly suggests, "Das must be read as a religious poet."[17] While Das's melioritic vision draws upon the concept of religion as a binding force furnishing to the good of humanity, she is also aware of the spiritual element in religion. Her poetic vision, at once, gazes into the soul and to the teeming humanity at large. Kamala Das, the Janusfaced poet, bears the quality of Wordsworth's wisest philosopher: she is "true to the kindred points of Heaven and Home".

References

1. Radhakrishnan, *Eastern Religions and Western Thoughts*, Oxford: Clarendon Press, 1939, pp. 19, 21.
2. All references to Kamala Das's poetry, unless otherwise mentioned, are from *Only the Soul knows How to Sing*, Kottayam: DC Books, 1999.
3. W.K. Wimsatt, 'Genesis: A Fallacy Revisited', in David Newton-de Molina (ed.), *On Literary Intention*, Edinburgh: Edinburgh University Press, 1976, p. 136.
4. *The Bhagavad Gita*, (trans.) P.Lal, Delhi: Hind Pocket Books, 1965, p. 89.
5. Kamala Das, *A Writers Predicament*, March 12, 1981, p. 2. Presented to the author by the poet as a manuscript.
6. Kamala Das, 'Sex: Mindless Surrender or Humming Fiesta', *Femina*, June 6, 1975, p.19.
7. Fritz Blackwell, 'Krishna Motifs in the Poetry of Sarojini Naidu and Kamala Das', *Journal of South Asian Literature*, Vol. 13, No. 1—4, 1978.

8. *Mundaka Upanishad,* III.2.8.
9. http://en.wikipedia.org/wiki/Kamaladas.
10. 'How I Embraced Islam' in www.islamicbulltin.org/newsletter/issue, 19.
11. Quoted in Margaret Chatterjee, 'Religious Pluralism in the Indian Context", in Eliot Deutsch (ed.), *Culture and Modernity: East-West Philosophic Perspectives,* Delhi: Motilal Banarasidass Publishers, 1994, p. 394.
12. *Al Harmony* Vol. 6, July/Sept. 2005. No pagination.
13. Anthony Perera, 'Love India, love Sri Lanka', *Sunday Observer,* April 29, 1984. No pagination.
14. The Holy Quran, (trans.), Abdullah Yusuf Ali, Hertfordshire: Wordsworth Editions Limited, 2000, p. 76.
15. Ibid., p.147.
16. 'The many journeys of Kamala Das', M.S. Unnikrishnan, Spectrum, *The Tribune,* March 4, 2007. No pagination.
17. Vincent O' Sullivan, 'Whose Voice is Where? On Listening to Kamala Das', S.C. Harrex and Vincent O' Sullivan (eds.), *Kamala Das—A Selection with Essays on Her Work,* Adelaide: CRNLE, 1986, p.187.

8

Feminine Sensibility in the Poems of Kamala Das

—Muktha Manoj Jacob

"To be seen and not heard" (Beauvoir, de, Simon 22) had been the fate of the Indian women for a long time. Das, however, "burst upon the Indo-Anglican scene like a darting, fascinating spectre of unconventionality blasting the traditional reticence's of Indian womanhood" (Daruwalla, 98). Her poetry is not merely Indian but a passionate expression of the universal experience of love, despair, anguish and failure apprehended through a feminine sensibility which, is also Indian. Thus we have the beginning of the genre of feminine criticism which represents the discovery of a voice, a unique and powerful voice capable of cancelling those other voices.

Born and brought up in a traditional Nair family of Kerala, Kamala Das writes about a world that she is familiar with. She writes about its customs, manners, rituals and traditions. In this society, she has a role of an insider-outsider in a sense that she belongs to it but at the same time she has travelled outside this social world and had enough exposure to other socio-cultural systems. It may be noted that just by expressing her thoughts; she is actually attacking the mores of a society that believes in *silence of women.*

As a feminine writer Das is riddled with emotions at the plight of the woman in a patriarchal society. In India where rape, dowry deaths, female infanticide, and various other forms of exploration are almost every day happenings, the female consciousness cries out for articulation. Even the birth of a girl child is unwelcome.

Patriarchy, which forms the major target of Kamala Das's attack, is cnly one form among several hierarchies that oppress *Indian women*. Even the Indian Constitution declares women along with the former untouchables and tribals to be recognised as weaker section of society.

It is against this unique social background that I attempt to discuss the feminist sensibility in Kamala Das's poems. Whereas feminist anger in the West may be seen as a woman's cry against the hypocrisy of a culture that accords centrality to the values of equality and individual freedom, though denies equality to women, the situation in India is different in that both men and women have hitherto functioned under rigid hierarchies, learned to crush freedom, conditioned themselves to suppress their needs, silence their senses and sublimate their cells in a philosophy of self-denial, self-effacement and services.

Kamala Das is an Indian in every sense of the word. She was born in India and her writing reveals her Indiananess and her patriotism. As a woman bilingual writer in a postcolonial society, she marks her protest through a strong resistance to authoritarian orthodoxy, and deliberately demolishes all conventional, structures. Her subjective self thus enters her poetry. The body serves as the catalyst. She, like other women poets, uses a language that is more frank, more pervasive. Wallace Grabbe observes that Das's poetry "fights against and is to some extent, a product of multiple displacement" (Ravindran, 198)

Firstly, displacement felt over the loss of "tradition". Secondly, the language and thirdly, the displacement she experiences on account of being a woman. Kamala Das attempts to hold on to the tradition with the help of her memory, which gets back to her childhood. She had a cloistered existence as a child surrounded by loving relatives and loyal servants. In her autobiographical book in Malayalam *Balyakalasmarankal* she recreates her childhood experiences. She writes about her grand uncle Nalapat Narayanana Menon, whose literary genius inspired her. She also recalls the time when her uncle gave her Walt Whitman's collection of poems to read. It is therefore not surprising that Das became a famous writer.

However what is surprising is that she has been writing in English and that too in a frank and open manner about issues not generally discussed in a 'polite' society. Her autobiographical/ fictional work in English *My Story* is "a document expressing the writer's own ambiguity as a woman asserting subjective power in the traditional society" (Sherley Geok). This book not only fascinated readers but also invited severe criticism as her female self completely challenged the conventional socio-cultural perception in India. Her personal experience has shown her how weak females are when confronted by dominating men.

In an unpublished letter to her sister she writes about how helpless she felt when her father found a husband for her and fixed her marriage without any consideration for her feelings:

> ...I was persuaded to marry, and I had no courage to refuse to do what even my father wanted me to do. I have not shown by a word or sign, that I felt trapped, let down and disillusioned... (To Sulochana, July 1958)

Das has the ability delve deep into her consciousness and to create female images, which are at once her and that of the other women. As she uses her personal voice to speak on behalf of others, it results in the identification of her person with the persona in her writing. This is the cause for a lot of misunderstanding and it even brought her a fair measure of notoriety. In spite of all the adverse publicity, her family has stood by her through thick and thin which is expressed in the poem "Daughter", written by Das's mother, Balamani Amma,

> ....
> Your power of turning worms into butterflies comforts me.
> (198)

The world believes in two creeds of humanity – the masculine and the non-masculine. The woman has been seen "other" the "lesser" and weaker in contrast to the male who is in every way "superior". This attitude has been established and perpetuated ever since the Middle Ages, starting with the theory of the creation of woman from the "rib" of Adam. This unfortunate belief has continued to be in existence to the present day.

Women have been forced to believe that their duty lies in staying within the house. Of late, however, women have started voicing their protests. But Kamala Das personally feels, for a woman, her husband and family are equally important than her career. However, her poems are feminine urges and passion brought out in powerful myths. Her sense of identity is so fragile that she thinks there are many "I's" reciding within her every thought and impulse claiming its own identity. She proclaims: "I am sinner, I am saint, I am the beloved and the betrayed. I have no joys which are not yours, no aches which are not yours. I too call myself "I" ("An Introduction", 26).

Kamala Das's narrative begins with a mention of the dawn of early consciousness of her political have-nots, the awareness that she belonged to an oppressed race .As a little child growing up in Calcutta, she was made aware that her brown skin was a disadvantage to her which was ruled by white men. She would resent being part of a race which was colonised. Dark complexion was associated with inferiority while the white colonisers were regarded as a superior race. Bearing the burden of a swarthy skin, she entered adolescence in the pre-independence days, feeling helpless and frustrated, harboring a grudge against the British who ruled over India and treated them as slaves.

. At the same time there was oppression in the domestic and social spheres too. In Kamala Das's family, the system of matriarchy was followed. Not that it differed much from patriarchy because power politics in matriarchy is not very much different from that of patriarchy. The different lies in that male power is passed on to a next generation to a female descendant. Hence, Kamala Das's uncle was the head of the clan. Her mother was more or less indifferent to what went on around her, preferring to spend most of her time writing poetry in Malayalam. Her father ruled supreme. He would lay down the rules of the family insisting that they be followed. She remembers how he would "roar" and how rough his hands were when he forced her and her brother to swallow castor oil. "He had warned me that if I did not do well in Maths, he would marry me off. Unfortunately, I did not do well in Maths and hence I was married off as a punishment" (1984, Interview).

Sex in the Nair community that Das grew up in was an unmentionable topic and to add to it child marriage was prevelant. (Her marriage – very early at the age of fifteen).

Her relationship with her husband "was like a chieftain who collected the taxes due to him from his vassals, simply" (Kamala Das, 98)

This husband represents the patriarchal society which wishes to see women only in submissive roles

> Dress in sarees, Be girl
> Be Wife, they said. Be embroiderer, be cook,
> Be quareller........
> Choose a name, a role. Don't play pretending games
> ("An Introduction")

Marriage places before a woman a set of gender defined roles inscribed by society. Transgressing these roles is tantamount to a defiance of social norms and invites a wrath of the power holders, in this case the men. Reality, for the society is only what it chooses to see and it chooses to see women in certain fixed roles. Thus a woman is forced to wear a mask throughout her life, whether she relishes or not:

> I must pose
> I must pretend
> I must act the role
> Of happy woman
> Happy wife ("'The Suicide")

This is how society wishes to see its women: as happy wives and mothers content in the greater glory of father/husband/lover. Women, have no business to be discontented with their lot. Kamala Das however, protests:

Woman, Is this happiness, this lying buried
Beneath a man? It's time again to come alive
The world extends a lot beyond his six-foot frame
("The Conflagration")

The idea of being buried alive, of being smothered in a claustrophobic world runs through her poetry and she longs to escape from it:

I shall someday leave, leave the cocoon
You built around me with morning tea,
....I shall someday take
Wings, fly around, as often petals
Do when free in air"
(I Shall Some Day - *Summer in Calcutta*)

The desired movement is from captivity to liberation as a woman (wife rather) seeks her own space. It is captivity in the domestic setup that the poet finds dissatisfying. It does have love in some form but only in the form of tidbits, only as a jaded, indifferent emotion. This is a kind of sentiment present in most Indian arranged marriages that keep a woman duty-bound to her home. It may provide security, at the same time "Secures" her firmly to a place patriarchy inscribes for her. There are few other options available to her. Her concern is not only with her personal predicament but with that of all women trapped in a love/ marriage relationship which refuses to let women grow as independent entities. She seems to address no one particular man but all men in general who take for granted that women must play a subservient role and that their lives must revolve around their male partners. "Cowering/beneath your monstrous ego I ate the magic loaf and became a dwarf" (*The Old Playhouse and Other Poems*)

She must live her life as a pigmy, in the shadow of her husband who looms large over her life. It is his world in which she has been condescendingly given a small inconsequential place.

Kamala Das's attempt is to move from margin to centre from a position of little to no consequence to one which is crucial to her world. Hence, she shifts her focus from women as the representatives of a patriarchal power to a woman as a separate self. In a bid to tell the male world that she cares little for them or their authority, she turns to herself and becomes conventional.

A powerful desire for freedom and a freedom to rebel forms a central strain in several of her poems. These characteristics are derived from her Nair lineage, and are effectively modulated and channellised by the influence of education and the awareness of the feminist protest against male domination. The urge to fly into the endless pathways of the sky finds expression occasionally in thunderous outbursts against the male world represented by her husband and in wiled deprecation of the symbols of the male tyranny in obscene language. But usually the protest is a well-known contrived artifice aimed at securing sympathy for her rather than creating antipathy towards the male.

While Das experiences rage and anger very often at the sad plight of the common woman, there are times when she is overcome by feelings of despair and helplessness. Then it appears as if she feels things are not going to change, and she becomes a fellow sufferer almost defeated by the cruel society and its pretensions. Such a state of mind can be discerned in poems such as "Of Calcutta" where she ruefully depicts her laws of liberty stemming from marriage.

> I was sent away to protect family's
> Honor, to save a few cowards; to defend some
> ....A mother for his sons, yet another nodding
> Doll for his parlour, a walkie-talkie, one two
> Warm his bed at night" (*Collected Poems,* 59).

In another poem Kamala Das writes that her whole world is roofed by "hostile skies" ("The Stranger and I, Soul", 39) and that the male does not see her with eyes but "with hands". Poems such as these dramatise her aching disappointment rather than a burning rage.

In Das's poetry we have sadness, anger, rebellion, at times, despair and hopelessness and above all that is her unfailing optimism. She is sure that there is light at the end of the tunnel and the condition of woman is bound to change. The humiliation of being treated as a sexual object and vassal in the house underlined for her the shallowness of the marital bond. Her rebellion against the requirement to become domesticated, to cater to the master whenever necessary and to be on display as a showpiece can be seen in her poems "Descendants" and "Substitute".

Kamala Das protests against the marginalisation of women and social injustices and communicates a powerful female sensibility in her poetry. Her self-assertion is clear in her "An Introduction" (1965) in which she speaks in the guise of a sixteenyearsold girl who rebels against the norms of patriarchal society to defend and secure her identity in the world. Her defence against patriarchal dictation of don't write in English (An Introduction) presents a passionate defense not only for writing in English but also for writing in Indian English—the English one is comfortable with and in which she writes. She craves for artistic and personal freedom of expression in the matters of language, form, subject and style.

As language parameter is a kind of cage which makes one unable to express true emotions and feelings, one needs to choose a language for expression for self and in this way one's own choice of words for selfexpression and selfattainment. Naturally there is rising voice of depression, frustration and anger against any control or restriction imposed on her. She utters firmly and confidently: "The language I speak, Becomes mine, its distortions, its queerness All mine, mine alone. It is half-English, half- Indian, funny perhaps, but it is honest, It is as human as I am human, don't You see"? (*An Introduction,* p 23)

Kamala Das is generally seen in the forefront of such writers who fought for the rights of women. She writes in her poem:

> Father, I ask you now without fear, Did you want me
> Did you ever want a daughter"? ("Next to Indira Gandhi")

She becomes the supporter of women who have been oppressed and trampled for centuries. She crosses the patriarchal stronghold and tells boldly what women suffer silently—the story of her quick growth into puberty, her sudden marriage, her first sexual encounter in a closed room on the wedding night, etc. She criticises the institutions of marriage which gives a man a legal right to commit marital rape on his teenage bride. She rebels impulsively and defies the gender code. She dresses herself in shirts and trousers, cuts her hair short and sits on walls. She refuses to fit in the constructed role of "a girl", "a wife". She does wish to become a woman by wearing saris. Like her own language, she chooses her own man. The poem completes with a strong note of self-assertion: "I too call myself I" ("Next to Indira Gandhi") an assertion of her individual-self, her independent-self and her integral-self.

She refuses to be weak and passive and self-less, self-denying, sacrificing and a compliant angel under a masculine value system. She speaks against all kinds of dominance, oppression and asserts the need of sanity in human relation which is the only mode of preservation of human existence on this planet. Her poem "The Sunshine Cat" presents an attractive, sensitive and creative woman caught in a loveless marriage suffers a nervous breakdown and becomes a cold, halfdead woman now of no use at all to men. To her the tragedy of 'life is not that' 'man dies' but 'love dies'. She opposes all gender bias which distances men from women and discriminates between them. She reveals the unimportance of gender or the classification into "he" and "she":

> When a man is dead, or a woman
> We call the corpse not he
> Or she but it ("Descendants", 16)

To Kamala Das masculinity and feminity are the traits of one's personality which transcends gender barriers based on biological and social identity. Her poems assume their location, create their space by being set in situations rather than by observing or alluding to their environment. In the end I can say that there is a split-self and selfassertion in the poetry of Kamala Das. Almost all the collection of her poetry speak aloud for the cause of woman but she is not only the champion of the rights of woman but she also torch bears the path of modern woman, who has been blind folded by the extreme light of Westernisation and modernisation. Knowing very well that spirituality will offer her solace:

> In 1999 she converted to Islam, an action she said she had been contemplating for many years. She said, in an interview with a leading Malayalam newspaper, "Two plain reasons lured me to Islam One is the Purdah. Second is the security that Islam provides to women. In fact, both these reasons are complementary. Purdah is the most wonderful dress for women in the world. And I have always loved to wear the Purdah. It gives women a sense of security. Only Islam gives protection to women. I have been lonely all through my life. At nights, I used to sleep by embracing a pillow. But I am no longer a loner. Islam is my company. Islam is the only religion in the world that gives love and protection to women. Therefore, I have converted (Interview to the Malayalam Newspaper, *Kerala Koumati*)

Ramchandran Nair rightly points out the reality in Kamala Das's poems:

> Kamala Das's voice is the voice of anguish. Nevertheless, she has been exhibiting intense faith in the worth and value of life. There is neither pessimism nor sentimentalism in her poetry. A vigorous sense of life and a virile faith in the glory and beauty of human endeavours inhabit her poetry.
>
> (Ramachandran Nair, p.138)

Works Cited

Balamani, Amma, "To My Daughter", *Indian Poetry Today,* Vol.4. New Delhi, Indian Council for Cultural Relations, 1981.

Based on the Report that appeared in *Malayala Manorama* Internet edition on 12th Dec. 1999.

Daruwalla, Kaki (ed.), *Confessional Poetry as Social Commentary,* India, Vikas Publishing House, 1980.

Das, Kamala, Letter to Sulochana: based on the Report that appeared in *Malayala Manorama* Internet edition on 26th July 1986.

– *My Story,* New Delhi, Sterling, 1988.

De Beavoir Simon. *The Second Sex* (rpt) London, Piccador, 1988.

De Souza Eunice, (ed.), *Nine Indian Women Poets,* Delhi, Oxford University Press, 1997.

Geok Shirley, "Terms Of Empowerment in Kamala Das's My Story", In *Decolonising the Subject : The Politics Of Gender In Womens' Autobiography* (ed.), Julia Watson, pp. 369. University of Minnesota Press, 1992.

Nair Ramachandran, *The Poetry Of Kamala Das,* New Delhi, Reliance Publishing House, 1993.

Raveendran, P.P. (ed.), "Text as History, History as Text: A Reading of Kamala Das's Annamalai Poems", *A Journal of Commonwealth Literature,* Vol.29 No.2 pp. 47-54.

Sanghavi Malavika, Women at her Best: An Interview recorded at IBH Mahalaxmi Chambers, Bombay, 1984.

9

An Obsessive Self is Seeking Freedom: A Study in Kamala Das's Poetry

—Bikram Kumar Mohapatra

Kamala Das (1934-2009), whose voice counts the much credible moments of bloodshedding in pity, the experience of life in fullness without self propaganda, dry and lifeless ego and who draws the picture from the deep fathomless corner of life, has become the most discussed name in Indian English literature. She has no comparison with her contemporaries to reveal the internal moods and feelings of a woman with much courage and honesty. She is widely acclaimed as a unique artist for her symphony, her leftist approach against the maledominated society. The male domination on feminine psyche, when participated in the world of nature, has ignited her mind to revolt against the establishment and to set her status in a way of individual freedom. She has become a mouthpiece of all women, suppressed and suffered in a male hegemonic set up. She needs the justice of equality and fulfilment. In this way her tone in her poems becomes heavy and the confessional elements rush in to the realm of reality to explore a kind of new canvas which is fit for her thought and approach.

In the beginning of her creative career she was known as Madhavi Kutty when she was writing in Malayalam; then she became known as Kamala Das, a popular poet in Indian English literature. But in 1999 she accepted Islamic religion and became Kamala Suraiya and passed away in May 31, 2009 at the age of 75. However, her life has became a prominent voice in her poetry with a professed confessional spectrum. She will be better remembered for it because it is as a poet she excels herself here.

The real power of expression of an artist lies with the unconditional pronouncement of self. It has a different glow everywhere and at every time. An essential quality of any writing is the reflection of selfindulgence. That is the reason of the latest insight and sharpness of approach, because the language of such writing enlivens the known experience of the reader and awakes his sentiment. Later on it encompasses the reader's attachment and leads to a greater melancholic state. The taste of life and its pronouncement easily control the mind of the reader. She sustains the commitment to write the tremor from the depth of life and its sheer delight in her poetry. It is for that she selects and arranges the linguistic elements that evoke the right kind of emotion.

Indian English poetry of today has come though a long way tradition with observation and analysis shifted from the romantic, socio-cultural and spiritual–transcendental scroll to a new kind based on personal experience. The exposure of a private voice sustains the magnitude in new poetry. A group of poets like P. Lal, Nissim Ezekiel, A.K. Ramanujan, Shiv. K. Kumar, Pritish Nandi, Kamala Das, Mamata Kalia, Gouri Deshpande, De Souza and Jayanta Mahapatra, etc., explored personal tone in poetry as a new device. More or less these poets accept the dominant confessional mode in poetry. This mode finds an important place providing the reader a proper perspective. This mode also approves the quest for identity and rootedness in poetry with the aptness of imagery and diction.

To hide the truth without its expression is definitely an unpardonable crime that kills our instinctual honesty. An artist writes with his pen to express the truth, not to hide it. Certainly the truth is illuminated with the appreciation of art. Confession is not an art, rather it is a decorative form of an art. It reveals the internal life of an artist. It does not get its right form until and unless the internal life is revealed. Though the term 'confession' has prevailed since the days of Augustine and before, the confessional poets used a new phrase coined by M.L. Rosenthal while reviewing Robert Lowell's *Life Studies*. He states, the term 'confessional poetry' comes naturally to mind, "whoever invented it, it was a term both helpful and too limited, and very possibly the conception of a confessional school has by now done a certain amount of damage" (25). But towards the early 1970s confessional poetry got its official recognition while different universities in Europe organised the workshop on poetry therapy. The use of idiom, thought and technique is something different here. The poets express the unconscious state through the emotions, which are always true to their own feeling. These poets are very much sensitive towards the conflicts and problems of their inner life. In this way the portrait of frankest selfrevelations in art is offered to the public creating a general awareness of human nature.

In the second half of the twentieth century a group of American poets started writing on a highly subjective matter. The expression of personality without escape bloomed in the poems. The emotional content appears personal rather than impersonal. In the narrative content the protagonist seems to be unbalanced, afflicted or alienated. This group of poets includes Robert Lowell, John Berryman, W.D. Snodgrass, Theodore Roethke, Anne Sexton and Sylvia Plath to establish the confessional pattern in poetry. The new poets in India writing in English initiated their voice in poetry in a manner that resembled with that pattern. They used the self as a poetic symbol around which hover a personal mythology. Among them Kamala Das excels the position. She started writing in open form and in open language. Her poetry especially displays moral courage with anti establishment in content and alienation in common theme.

Kamala Das's creativity is enriched with the conflicts of self in a broad spectrum of experiences that she gathers from Malabar where she lived first, and from the metropolitan cities like Calcutta, Bombay and Delhi later on. She has published eleven books of poems in her mother tongue and three books of English verse. Her collections of English poems include *Summer in Calcutta* (1965), *The Descendants* (1967) and the *The Old Play House* (1973). She was also collaborated with Pritish Nandi in a collection of love poems, *Tonight, This Savage Rite* (1979). The other collections of her best poems are collected poems : Volume – I, *The Best of Kamala Das*, edited by P.P. Raveendran and *Only The Soul Knows How to Sing*, selections from Kamala Das. All these poems provided her a wide recognition creating a newmode in Indian English poetry and a new taste for the readers.

Kamala Das emerged from a vast poetic tradition of women writing in English. It stretches back to the pioneers like Toru Dutta, Aru Dutta and Sarojini Naidu. She was also influenced by the tribal songs of her early inhabitants, the sangam poets of Tamil, the devotional poets of the middle age like Mirabai and by the celebrated malayali poet Balamani Amma, her mother. Das also imbibed her local tradition of the Malabar poets with her own ancestry of Nalapat House. Her poetic sensibility for English language poetry was enriched with her native roots.

The spirit of Indo–English poetry in pre-independent period sustained with the issues of nationalism and mostly the metaphysical preoccupation. Poetry appears to be enriched with the factors of decolonisation or a perpetual dialogue with the eternity. It may resemble with the Victorian romanticism. But the modern Indian English poetry has become a post-independence phenomenon. A new kind of idiom was used suited to the native sensibility and the postcolonial conception developed in the mind set of the poet. The new poets rejected the ossified remains of the colonial past. A new body of poetry came out with contemporary life. As Bruce King remarks:

> Poetry of the pre-independence period was, the writers felt, a mass of sentiments, clutches, out dated language and conventions the ossified remains of colonial tradition badly in need of a new start through grafting on a vital body of contemporary verse and contact with contemporary life and speech (11).

The new poets in India like, Das, concentrated in contemporary life with the revelation of self. Some of these poets write with the allusions to their life and the desire for personal change but Kamala Das brings forward her private life as the subject matter. Her poems are highly emotive, self-revelatory, moody and more confessional. They are treated with the realised settings and deeper feelings. The intensity of her emotion does not go beyond the complexity of life. Her feelings of loneliness, disappointment and obsessiveness contribute the part of her personality creating a game of selfhood. The anguished woman in Das stimulates her poetic self. She is marginalised. Like the rebirth of the phoenix, her artistic recreation occurs only when she dies to her human self.

The rebirth of the bird in the situation has become the sequel of the ashes as the remnant afflicted past made a potent influence on Das's artistic orientation. Despite the highly intellectual family set-up she received only a negligible amount of formal education. She was forced to marry even before her sixteenth birthday by her autocratic father. She found her husband nonchalant and lustful who was involved with the extra-marital relationship. His contact with her became cruel and brutal. Due to the lack of caring "she grew revengeful towards him, and reacted in a non-traditional fashion in love making, offering herself to any handsome or resourceful man who come across her, and forgiving even her rapist" (Dwivedi 2). As a wife she slashed her ego and became rebellious, angry and confused turning towards others for affection. Her broken marriage had become a setback, a blow to her ego but in contrast it became a blessing in disguise as her accumulated condensed emotion got a way for oozing out in an artistic vein. Regarding her "flopped" marital status she remarks in her most discussed about biographical exposition, *My Story:*

> I could not admit to all that my marriage had flopped. I could not return home to the Nalapat House, a divorcee for there had been good-will between our two families. . . . A broken marriage was as distasteful, as horrifying as an attack of leprosy. If I had at that time listened to the dictates of my conscience and had left my husband, I would have found it impossible to find another who would volunteer to marry me, for I was not conspicuously pretty and besides there was the two-year-old who would have been to the new husband an encumbrance (102)

Though she became a dwarf woman now almost entirely at the mercy of her husband the sturdy walls of the matrimonial structure cracked by the mismatching mind but a longing for feminine zest with endless female hunger made her an investigator for passion and passionate bond. She has written a number of poems exploring pain and frustration. Within the confinement of domestic walls she recreates her artistic self, the second self of a woman. There is a fundamental relationship between her autobiographical self and artistic self. Her poetic journey of Kamala Das leads with a capital of nativity, a postcolonial agenda. She assumes the idea in her poem "An Introduction":

> I am an Indian, very brown, born in
> Malabar, I speak three languages, write in
> Two, and dream in one. Don't write in English, they said
> English is not your mother tongue why not leave
> me alone, critics, friends, visiting cousins,
> Every one of you? Why not let me speak in
> Any language I like? The language I speak
> becomes mine. (5-12)

The subaltern accepts English as the native language. Here the post colonial feminist question of identity is not a blur. Despite the protest she identifies English as a poetic medium and an inseparable component of Indian identity. In an alien tongue mimicry is validated when there was ambivalence to use English for poetic preparation she creates her familiar attitude for this language as her native one.

The diction of Kamala Das is lyrical as weils as natural. Simplicity, lucidity, ecstasy, candid thoughts and clarity of expression are the hallmarks of her poetry. She does not create the iron curtain with philosophical brooding and mystical abstractions for the readers to enter into her poetic world. She uncovers the inner self at the moment of conflict with the openness of thought and approach. Her problems are indigenous and centripetal. They are converted to the poetic ingredients. Despite her inclination to the erotic longings with the accompaniment of love, sexual hunger, warmth of the body and compassion, the psychic dilemma that originates from the domestic displeasure, act as a motivating force for her creativity. She affirms:

> I asked for love, not knowing what else to ask
> For, he drew a youth of sixteen into the
> Bedroom and closed the door. He did not beat me.
> But my sad body felt so beaten.
> The weight of breasts and womb crushed me. I shrank
> Pitifully.

I am sinner.
I am saint. I am the beloved and the
Betrayed. I have no joys which are not yours, no
Aches which are not yours. I too call myself.
("An Introduction", 26-13, 57-60)

The line "I too call myself I" is very much powerful in her poetic process. Kamala Das becomes her own creation. Her autobiographical self merges with the poetic self. She is the artist who suffers in the domesticity. Her actual experience is totally found beyond her expectation. She is shocked by her husband's involvement in homosexual affair. In this incident she found the rejection of her womanliness. It is also narrated in her autobiographical sketch *My Story*. Her psychosomatic state gets its strength from the situation:

> At this time my husband turned to his old friend for comfort. They behaved like lovers in my presence. To celebrate my birthday, they should me out of the bedrooms and locked themselves in. I stood for a while, wondering what two men could possibly do together to get some physical rapture, but after some time, my pride made me move away. I went to my son and lay near him. I felt then revulsion for my womanliness. The weight of my breasts seemed to be crushing me. My private part was only a wound, the soul's wound showing through (110).

In the long run her sufferings fuel the creation, though her distinct personality becomes dwarf in the situation. She says:

You called me wife,
I was taught to break saccharine in to your tea and
to offer at the right moment the vitamins. Cowering
beneath your monstrous ego I ate the magic loaf and
became a dwarf. I lost my will and reason and to all your
questions I mumbled incoherent replies.
("The Old Play House", 12-17)

Her natural freedom is ceased; she becomes dwarf in the situation. She loses her reason and mirth but suggestively protests against the male ego and domination. She engages herself in the hectic search for love.

Kamala Das is dedicated to the celebration of love in all its aspects. She does not intellectualise it like all other confessional poets rather in her confessional tone she broods over profound emotion with richness of feeling. In her alienated poetic self love and passion merge with erotic influence. Though she does not use the wit and intelligence like Donne or the implicit intellectual current like Anne Sexton and Sylvia Plath, the attribution of erotic influence adds the strength to her poetry. She expresses her contentment in love:

> Until I found you
> I wrote verse, drew pictures,
> And went out with friends.
> For walks
> Now that I love you,
> Curled like an old mongrel
> My life lies content
> In you . . . . ("Love")

Sexual love is an initial sin in youth; it is attached to every life. Of course there is no such virtue in life. We all feel the gripping, moments with the beloved or the pangs of separation. In these moments we feel our instinct in tussle. But those who are involved in art practice and feel to be noble, don't feel it virtuous to reveal their real love in expression. In absorption, a true artist worships the demonic spirit to express the savagery of man, serpentine huger and other evolutionary facts of life.

The basic reformation of an artist lies with his truthfulness and universalisation. He expresses the reality and he never feels regret to be victimised for the cause. He does not remain in trepidation for honour rather revolts against injustice and truthlessness. Kamala Das is such a poet who unveils her own personal feelings with final disillusionment. Her love poems stem from profound anguish and very seldom from fulfilment. The anguish that originates from alienation gives birth the sad poems, even in her early age, about dolls that lost their heads and had to remain headless forever. Often she is misunderstood by her community, she feels isolation. Her premature marriage also isolated her from her beloved grandmother and Nalapat house. Her female persona is repeatedly betrayed in every possible way. In the woeful situation she asks herself: "women, is this happiness, this lying buried / Beneath a man? ("The Conflagration"). In "substitute" she counts life with blackmail and sorrow: "Life is quite simple now / love, blackmail and sorrow" (14-15) In "Losing Battle" she says:

> How can my love hold him when the other
> Flaunts a gaudy lust and is lioness
> To his Beast? Men are worthless, to trap them
> Use the cheapest bait of all, but never
> Love, which in a woman must mean tears
> And a silence in the blood.

Often her lonely state makes a potent influence on her creative mind. This loneliness is generated by her situation and it has become a recurrent theme in her poetry. In the poem like "Punishment in Kindergarten" she remembers her loneliness in the picnic day. By the hedge, she was watching the steel – white sun being alienated by the white children. In "Ghanashyam" she say "At three in the morning / I wake trembling from dreams of stark white loneliness / like bleached bones cracking in the desert run is my loneliness" (32-34). Her loneliness is basically psychological and it is originated from the experience of humiliations, domination and repugnant situation. In her poetic pilgrimage the tragic dream of selfhood is enacted with profound depth. In her autobiography as well as in her poems she has projected her ultimate reconciliation with the mystic communion. In this way the Radha Krishna myth in her poems needs a better inhabitation. In the poem "Krishna" she proclaims that she is encompassed with the physical body of Krishna and with his love words her "wise worlds din" is shut out. It is a kind of complete reunion:

> Your body is my prison, Krishna
> I cannot see beyond it.
> Your love words shut out the wise worlds' din.

In "Radha" she has evolved a melting point after a long waiting.

> Everything in me
> Is melting, even the hardness at the core
> O Krishna, I am melting, melting
> Nothing remains but you (6-10)

In the ultimate goal of her poetic pilgrimage her vision of love is saturated with the maturity and lies unbeaten in the melting point. This love is both emotional and spiritual. Though her love poems bear the camouflage of erotica, there is a sustained undercurrent of reformation and rejection of sexual violence in her other poems. Her other poems like "A Hand like Bonsai", "Feline", "Fathima", "Wards", "After words", "The Dalit Panther". "Inheritance", "The Flag" and many others portray the themes having moral, social or patriotic value. But in her poems one cannot find the elaborate description of nature. Also she is not a poet of nature in the traditional sense of the term. Though she has employed the natural objections in her poetic canvas, she does not generate the flight of imagination, like the Romantics, from profane to spiritual or the description of the glory of nature in a broader sense. In the mode of her poetic praxis the description embodies with the unfaltering human situation.

The note of subjectivism is very much strong in the poetry of Kamala Das. She is concerned with the situation as a victim. Her indignation is germinated from the violence in the name of religion and race. She receives a sense of eternal torture. The chaos of psychic situation becomes the foreground of her poetry. She remains alert to kill the "dreadful dragons of dream and experiences" in her reoriented art. As Robert Phillips remarks:

> All confessional art whether poetry or not, is a means of killing the beast which are within us, those dreadful dragons of dreams and experiences that must be hunted down cornered, and exposed in order to be destroyed (2) In the exercise of self expression a confessional poet ventilates the sensationalised strains following the emotional revolutionary thoughts. In this way Das also expresses her personality "Moreover, confessional poetry is an expression of personality rather than an escape from it" (Phillips 9).

A nihilistic and corrosive meaning peeps through her expression. The chief sources of her poetry are a recurrent hunting of her childhood memories, her living surrounding with social reality and chiefly her body. Recollection of past has an ironic glint in the context of her poems. Very often she lives on her memory and accounts the incidents related with her grandmother, old house and childhood days then she leaps on to new poetic subjects. Social reality provides her a psychic trauma for its hard bridled but outworn principles. She develops her characteristic protest to leap across the situation for her liberated self. In fact, a great deal of her artistic relevance springs from the aura of her body. The cynic applauded her recognising as the queen of erotica or pornographic, a dubious distinction which is made with the consideration of only physical love and lust in her works. It is a fact that libido in any form of art attracts the sardonic attention. Due to the superficial assessment the nobility of work lost its significance. However in analysis, human condition as well as the philosophy of body should not be ignored. Kamala Das decorates her poetic pyramid sustaining the vestibule of unresolved tension, the conflict between desire and spasm, dream and reality. In the psycho-analytical framework her poetic contents oscillate between fulfilment and unfulfilment in love. The intensity of inner depravity, inadequacy and frustration along with the superficial joy has become the significant mark of human character in her most discussed poem "The Dance of Eunuchs". The eunuchs become the metaphor of suppressed desire:

> Long braids flying, dark eyes flashing, they danced and
> They danced, oh, they danced till they bled........
> ....
> Some beat their drums, others beat their sorry breasts
> And wailed, and writhed in vacant ecstasy.
>
> (5-6, 11-12)

In this regard K.R.S. Iyengar remarks: "Love is crucified in sex, and sex defiles itself and again and again. Life is a cruel mocking bird, like the Dance of the Eunuchs" (677). Her introspective vision centers round the truth of life which is adequately honest, lively and equally explosive.

Kamala Das soared into eminence in the mid-sixties with her gamut of feelings, parlance creating such an ambit of new phenomena in Indian English poetry. In global literature the novelists like D.H. Lawrence, Albert Moravia, Emil Zola, Vladimir Navkov, etc., have drawn the clear picture of the energy of love that leads a man towards the perfection with honesty, sacrifice and truthfulness. The evolutionary affinities between man and woman, the anthropological emotion for sex have the significant expression in Kamala Das's poetry that deserves the aesthetic value. She transcends the barrier of sex. She talks more about women because they are more exploited and oppressed then man. In her creative consciousness she deals with the aspects of human behavior. Her life is her poetry as Kafka, the French writer, declared that his life is literature, there is no artificial or falsification. Recollection of her past, alienation, love and death are the very fabric of her poetry. The spirit of her poetry comes through the discourse of woman's body language from the point of view of woman with the startling images and metaphors. Creating a fine poetic dome she breathed her last sigh recently on 31 May 2009. Her absence will create a vacuum in Indian English poetry for good.

WORKS CITED

Das, Kamala, *My Story*, New Delhi, Sterling Publishers Pvt. Ltd., 1976.

Dwivedi, A.N., *Kamala Das and Her Poetry*, Delhi, Doaba House, 1983.

Iyengar, K.R.S., *Indian Writing in English*, New Delhi, Sterling Publishers Pvt. Ltd, 2001.

King, Bruce, *Modern Indian Poetry in English*, Delhi, Oxford University Press, 1987.

Phillips, Robert, *The Confessional Poets*, London & Amsterdam, Fetter and Simons, 1973.

Rosenthal, M.L and M. Gall, *The Modern poetic Sequence, The Genesis of Modern Poetry*, New York: Oxford University Press, 1983.

10

Kamala Das's Poetry of Protest, Throes and Woes of Love

—Shobha Diwakar

> Woman, is this happiness, this lying buried
> Beneath a man? ... time again to come alive
> The world extends a lot beyond his six-foot frame.

"'From Possession' to 'Person' is the graph of a woman's journey that has given her experiences and with these experiences she explores the future possibilities for her fruitful contribution in the era of globalisation"(Arora).

Kamala Das, the rebel feminist, a postmodernist, is certainly not a voice in the wilderness. Her poetic energy bursts forth with introspective speculations. This inwardness and conscious feelings, churned confidently and unceremoniously, bitterly wrung our from the heart, is most apparent in poems such as "An Introduction" where she unabashedly writes about being crushed under "The weight of my breast and womb"(l.30), and confesses towards the end, "I am sinner, / I am saint. I am the beloved and the / Betrayed."

A bilingual writer, Kamala Das has remained a controversial figure because of her beliefs, disbeliefs and her bohemian lifestyle. Yet, setting aside her life, which presents a mirror-image in her poems; a Sahitya Academy winner, She is ostensibly a widely read popular poet, who writes her poems with vigour and vitality. This disconsolate poet hires her readers to her very own creative expressions like "bind of stone", "make holes in memory." "Sorry breasts", that reveals her abounding creativity. A nonconformist to the core, Das widely differs from her predecessors like Sarojini Naidu, Toru Dutt, and a host of her contemporaries like Eunice De Souza, Sumita Namjoshi, Sunita jain, Nomita Kalia, Imitiaz Dharker and Meena Alexander.

This paper analyses the resistance and protest embodied in Das's creativity, which has given her a global recognition: She is the only Indian woman who finds a place in the *Norton Anthology of Women Writers.*

All of Das' poems are honest revelations of her exploration of womanhood and love. Her collection of poems in *Summer in Calcutta* and *The Descendants* unveil the agony of lost love that most after leads to an erotic note appeal but the use of concrete words and images like "Corpse", "Maggots" must of sweat between breasts, "shock of menstrual blood", "female hungers" remain devoid of passion. The eroticism contained in these phrases are frank and unequivocal, as is the note of revolt. The idea contained in lines such as "..., ask me why his hands sway like a hooded snake / before ... my pupis..." or "...his limbs life pale and / Carnivorous plants reaching/out for me ..." ("The Stone Age") are not minced. She neither conceals not does she restrain the urge to expose her desires as a wife, a woman to satisfy the demands of her body which to her is not an inelegant subject to discuss. So she does not anchor her kindled passion on sophisticated bars to girder the loss she suffers from. For example she writes about her emptiness in lines such as "As empty as..., waiting/ Through long hours ......". Or what / If, he whispers stranger and / Hesitates at the gateway / Of my unfamiliar legs..." ("Freaks").

To Das, her husband is a crude brute who simply derives sadistic pleasures out of her abject suffering, and so afflicts more torture upon her. Men, to her are therefore "... toy-men of dust", whose "hands" are "like the withered boughs ..."("The House Buiders") and "are ... thin in limbs and dry...". ("The Dance of Eunuchs"). This disillusioned note is more overt in "Luminol" where she writes "Love-lorn.../ Luminous sleep banked in/ The heart of pills, for he shall not Enter / Your ruthless eve, / Being human clumsy .../ .

Although Das is an indian poet, she is first and foremost a woman. The gender she represents haunts her and the more she concentrates upon her being a woman the more avenues open for her voice of protest against the maledominated social setup. Her man, her husband, represents a class that enjoys stifling and shredding to bit, the 'womanliness'. Given a wider expression to this womanliness is what makes Das stand out as a poet of distinction—one who honestly attacks male chauvinism and grimly denounces the tortures forcibly suffered by all those women pigeon-holed in their homes under pretext of cultural and traditional pressures.

Anees Jung in her book *Unveiling INDIA: A Woman's Journey* poignantly writes "something unvoiced connects us – perhaps the simple fact that we are woman"(19). It is this 'unvoiced' connection that Kamala Das establishes through her grievances against male hegemony. This is again better understood by the following statement "to love and be loved symbolises to the traditional Indian woman her security, her happiness and her fulfillment" (Jung 19). Das seeks this "fulfilment" and poignantly conveys her thoughts when she writes "... I met a man, loved him ..., / He is every man / who wants a woman, just as I am every / woman who seeks love. / In him ..." ("An Introduction"). Elsewhere she writes "Getting a man to love you is easy / Only be honest about your wants as a / Woman". ("The Looking Glass").

In poems such as "The Dance of the Eunuchs" and "Jaisurya", Das writes about the agony of losing a child. The songs sung by the eunuchs are sad and melancholy because of the pain suffered by the loss of dying lovers and 'unborn' children. She writes: "....Their voices / were harsh, their songs melancholy they sang of / Lovers dying and of children left unborn ...." The lines reveal the emptiness of losses—their sterility and their helplessness. The same vacuity is echoed in other poems. That reverberates her emotional loss. This loss is conspicuously drawn in the following lines ".... I see you go away from me / And feel the loss of love I never once rec......" ("The Seashore"). Seemier Hasan writes, "Most of Kamala Das's poetry concerns itself with the poets intensely felt need fro declaring her intimate autobiography to the world ..." (Hasan, 25).

Thus, Das's poems reflect upon the predicament faced by a woman— whether it is the loneliness she suffers from or traumas created by her husband, another man / partner; or the loss of a child ("Jaisurya") ("The Dance of the Eunuchs"). Whatever it be, the tragedy envelops a woman like a dark cloud. The roaring, surging urges imprisoned within her 'self' are like 'adamantine Chains" (to use Milton's phrase from *Paradise Lost*), that bind a woman in marriage which turns to become a virtual Hell for her, and where, like Satan, she trudges on fiery ground to face the daily torments she is confronted with. Das's poetry demands liberation for women by breaking these 'Adamantine chains' in order to define their freedom from rigid societal taboos. A woman, as a wife has conscious needs that are deliberately crushed by oppressions. Das resists this marginalisation, and challenges these oppressions by demanding love. She writes, "I asked for love, not knowing what else to ask ..." ("An Introduction") and again, "You let your wife / Seek ecstasy in other's arms. ..." ("Conflagration"). She feels strangulated in these oppressive conditions and is tormented by "existential questions" pertaining to the "sphere of the reality of one's existence, the nature of freedom envisaged and the cause of failure in love ..." (Surendran 42). The cry is wrung out, "I must pretend, / I must act the role / Of happy woman, / Happy wife" ("The Suicide"). Das's uninhibited articulation may be attributed to her birth in a matrilineal setup of the Nair community where women were even allowed plurality of husbands.

Bruce King writes that postcolonial Indian poetry in English moved away from "such colonial and nationalistic themes as the reuniting of legends, praise of peasants, and from general ethical statements to writing about 'personal experience'" (147). Writing in postcolonial India that threw off the shackles of British oppressions, Das has effectively thrown off the shackles of male oppressions. She is, indeed, a liberated woman voicing her angst, her frustrations, her cries and her pains, suffered under the yoke of male hegemony. Exhibiting a "fiercely feminine sensibitlity", "her verse [is] a forum to voice the unexpected woes of womanhood that had long been hushed in silence. Her protest was not in vain rather it gave her an identity" (Iyengar, 680). Devendra Kohli writes that Kamala Das is "a poet of the modern Indian woman's ambivalence" (27). Hence, Das's poetry breathes in a new hope, which can gradually help woman to wriggle out of the alienation that smothers her inner vitality and desire to live life on her own terms.

Das's poetry is an amalgamation of love as a complex phenomenon that encompasses a multidimensional human experience. This experience especially revolves round the physical union of man and woman in marriage. A woman in India is brought up with cultural and sociological traditions, which to break or go against, is taboo. Nevertheless, in Das's poetry, the nectar of love and sex intermingle freely in poems like "Convicts", "The Sunshine Cat", "The Dance of the Eunuchs", "The Looking Glass" and "An Introduction", besides a host of others, which are like withered leaves upon the ground, browned and baked in the heat of the sun.

Das's passive retreat does not provide her any pleasure in physical union, because for her, no man could impart fulfilment to her hungry self. Whosoever she loved, demanded her body: her hollow soul remained tarnished for that touch—that tender human touch and understanding that would have made her soar like a bird in bliss. Perhaps the disillusioned tone of her poems reveals her 'scrupulous' honesty in revealing her 'self' unabashedly. In her confessional *My Story,* she asserts about her belief in 'being scrupulously honest to oneself' (195). Hence Das's creative genious searched for a meaning in life. Each time she hopes to cling, the moment slips off. Indeed, it seems as though all if her problems relate to her unhappy arranged marriage for which she was unprepared.

The traumas of this unhappy marriage constantly echo in Das's poetry. It is her tragedy of life that her husband did not care for her. This is evident in "Conflagration" where she writes candidly "... you let me loss my youth like coins / Into various hands, ... / ......, / You let your wife / Seek ecstasy in other's arms /". In *My Story* she narrates an incidence about the rough treatment she received on her return to Bombay from her brother's marriage. When she landed at Bombay airport her husband was not present to receive her. On request, a fellow passenger, her friend, gave her a lift. She reminiscences, "I ferlt lost and unwanted." Forlorn, she arrived home to find her children asleep, while her husband 'lazily' questioned her on being late. When Das reiterated sobbingly "Why didn't you come to the airport ...: Don't you love me at all?" Crudely he retorted, "I am tired and sleepy, we shall talk in the morning tomorrow..." (*My Story*, 126) Perhaps these neglects and verbal whips pervade Das's poems with rectitude.

Unlike Das who succumbed to an arranged marriage, Amrita Pritam, the renowned poet from Punjab, rebelled against it, choosing to live with a Muslim man she loved. She states, "Today a man and a woman sleep on a bed of bondage rather than of freedom. What kind of children can be borne if such a union?" (Qtd. in Jung, 66). Another woman (name undisclosed) bitterly remarks, "When I became his wife, I became his property .... He does not love me. He raped me every night. How can I say not to him? If I do I will be thrown out of the house." (Qtd. in Jung 67). It is precisely against this male knuckling down that Das vehemently protest. In the *Old Play House* she writes contemptuously about her role as a wife, "You called me wife, / .... /.... / convering/ Beneath your monstrous ego, I / Became a dwarf. I lost my reason and will, to all your/ Questions I mumbled incoherent replies." All these constraints strung round a woman's neck are traditionally taking to be dumb duty, which must be performed or the threat of being 'thrown out of the house', hangs like Duncan's Sword. It is against this dumb duty 'like breaking sacchame' into the tea and "offer at the right moment the vitamins" (*The Old Playhouse*), that Das raises her voice. Coupled with this artful performance is another duty that must be indulged into every night, behind closed doors. Her agony at this daily ordeal is revealed in "An Introduction" where she confesses "... he drew a youth of sixteen into the / Bedroom ..... / he did not beat me / But my dead woman-body felt so beaten ...." In "The Stone Age" she questions: "... Ask me why like / A great tree, felled, he slumps against my breasts, / And sleeps, ask me what is bliss and what its price." Elsewhere she writes ".. Tjos hacking at each other's pants / Like convicts hacking. / ... When he / And I were one, me were neither / male nor female." (*My Story*, Ch. 31). Yet it is true that Das, like any other teenage girl, entered marriage with multi-shaded hopes which were soon shattered, leading to undertones of disillusionment, which marks her major themes (M. Nirmala, 97). She writes:

Yes, I was thinking, lying beside him
That I loved, and was much loved.
It is a physical thing, he said suddenly,
End it, I cried, end it, and let us befull. ("Substitute")

Such intimate confessions abound in Das's poetry and the cry wrings out from the heart, "Ah, why does love come to me like pain / Again and again and again?" (*Only the Soul,* 136)

The reverberative echoing sound in 'again and again and again, 'are resurgent, as she turns to other men to satisfy her famished desires. This futile attempt, though repulsive, creates pity for a lonely heart in pursuit of 'love'; like Actacon, who falls victim to his men hounds, she too succumbs to her desires.

In spite of the fact that Das has revealed her intimate mental and physical in real like, she confessed, she was bored with love. Once after an argument with her husband she retorted, "But I let you make love to me every night, ... isn't that good enough?" Frankly she admits hat her husband was 'obsessed with sex' (*My Story,* 127-28). It is a different matter though that her autobiography, is after all only a story; a figment of the imagination. Intimate confessions in *My Story* reveal the disillusioned personality of Das and her unfathomable traumas. The loss of human relationship and that tender human touch she craved for all her life, consumed her robust energy in sucking freedom from the oppressions she endured through her ill-begotten marriage.

Das may be referred to as a 'radical feminist' (term borrowed from Singh, 107), who projected the male as one who derived pleasure in subjugating the female. Though his harsh tone raised towards the male is evidently more pronounced in Das's poetry, other modern poets write on a different note. Singh writes:

> Unlike Kamala Das and her contemporaries, the new woman poets hold and optimistic view of man-woman relationshship and refrain from pronouncing their humiliations, sexual repressions, frustrations and failure. (108).

Bashabi Fraser, a new poet, stands apart from Das's lamentations. Fraser views life, unlike Das, in all its colourful shades and accepts her role as a woman who willingly surrenders herself. She writes:

Yes, I'm life – the measure that
Touches the lips of man
And gives him his share of joy
And strife.... (Qtd. in Singh, 110)

In the foregoing lines, Fraser does not denounce physical union as abhorrent. She considers herself to be "life / Nectar for man". On the contrary for Das the limbs of man are like "...Carnivourous plants" ("In Love"). Like Fraser, Mona Dash also enjoys the company of her lover and unlike Das, enjoys the union. She writes:

I know this moment is only mine
Though you make it happen for me ...
I collapse, fall and rise,
Swim Dive, Fly
All in that instant. (Qtd. in Singh,115)

Fraser and Dash do not deny the pleasures of the flesh and hence there is no friction or conflict in their emotional revelation. Das, on the other hand does not resist the union but her carnal desires leave her hopelessly frigid; she writes:

... and, they said each of
Them, I do not love, ..., it is not
In my nature to love,
....., and in the evening when
He returned to take her out she was cold and
Half dead woman, now of no use at all to men.

("The Sunshine Cat")

Apparently it seems as though Das's intensive cravings fail to impart pleasure and hence, this lack of oneness, somewhere reveals an ego conflict that discolours her life. Despite seeking comfort in the arms of different men the image of her own husband lurk in the background. This ghostly shadow pursues her each time she seeks an extra-marital affair and perhaps this shadow curtails her enjoyment. She therefore remains a thirsty soul, always craving, always demanding more, to quench her unending lust' ("In Love").

As a poet, Das has fixed deliberations, motifs and patterns that run parallel in almost all her poems. As a woman the inward cry shrieks for sexuality. The barrier for rigid constraints to be borne only by the woman is deliberately crushed upon for this very demand. As such, the tone towards the male is hostile, hateful and denigrating. None of the poems discussed project the male as a lovable person. Perhaps the fact that Das was victimised not only by her own husband but also by all those men who used her for their own pleasure is the cause of this vituperation. This is evident in the following lines:

> They did this to her the men who knew her, the man
> She loved, who loved her not enough being selfigh
> And a coward, the husband who neither loved nor
> Used her, but was a ruthless Watcher ......
>
> ("The Sunshine Cat")

The incompatibility as partners in sexual union is more pronounced in her poem "Henons" written as far back as in 1960. Here she writes:

> On sedatives
> I am move lovalble,
> Says my husband ...
> ....
> And,
> My rag doll limbs adjust better to his vensabile lust....
>
> ("Henons")

A careful reading of Das's verse reveals the plight and harrowing experiences of a distressed soul, yearning to establish her own identity as a woman. Herein creeps in the collective experience of womanhood and thereby unleashes 'their' muted voice. So for Das "... Each truth / Ends.. with a f......"(Nani) even as the woman pretends to fulfil the role "of happy woman, / Happy life" ("The Suicide").

It may be analytically drawn that Das considers male supremacy in the act of physical union, as gender force. Like Jill Johnston she seems to assert that 'sexual ... between man and woman is an invasion of the woman, the woman does not get anything up to participate in the congress....' (Qtd. in Singh 146). This sense is truthfully conveyed in lines where Das writes how 'Nimble finger tips' cannot 'unleash' her or how her 'Body' is 'drab and destitute' and 'The heart,/ On enply .... Waiting / .... / (The Freaks) or "You turn me into a bird of stone, a granite / Dove," ("The Stone Age").

Das's provocati--e poetry, consumed with personal lamentations and intimate disclosures, has evoked critical reactions. A careful reading of Das's *My Story* mentions an encounter with a young girl against whom she was warned, to keep away (Chap 31). Das wondered why. Her curiosity was soon satisfied, when travelling together in the train this girl sneaked into her berth (when all else were fast asleep), and kissed her all over so passionately that it left her indelibly 'unnerved'. The softness with which this girl caressed her all night was "a gentleness that [she] had never dreamt of finding" (*My Story* 79). Does this revelation subtly bare the fact that Das herself was perhaps a lesbian and therefore her desires could never be fulfilled by her male partner? The rapturous touch the tenderness that Das recalls remained forever buried in some deep layers of her memory. Das confessed, "I met her, and felt instantly drawn towards her..." She further admits, "When her eyes held mine captive in a trance ... then I felt excited ,,, she was like and animal ... " (*My Story* 78). While this may be a far fetched statement, it could possibly spit out the truth about Das accusing Indian men of 'losing their masculinity" (Sing, 148).

Presumably, this was the tragedy of Das's sufferance, who breathed her last on May 31, 2009, in Pune. Probably she coined her own obituary when she wrote about the image of death and decay.

> O Sea, I am fed up
> I want to be simple
> I want to be loved
> And
> If love is not to be had
> I want to be dead, just dead.

As Das grew frail over the years, she remained infused with the idea of death, 'The youth' that was tossed "like coins / Into various hands / was engulfed in ... thoughts of death and decay".

Although Das's provocative verse has raised controversial responses, as a very modern poet she steps ahead of the

Aristotelian theory of poetry being a criticism of life. The resulting societal changes have not restrained her voice her alienation and subdued self to emerge out of the narrow domestic walls; to uphold her identity and individualism. Nevertheless, her sceptical and cynical accusations do distort the image of man and tantalise the readers' own ideology towards the opposite sex even though she is aware of the poet's own disintegrated personality.

Indeed Das's traumatised experiences are like the fissured wounds of the cracked, dried up earth, the gashes of which, open, dry and aching, shriek out for a cool drop of nectar from heaven that would soother its bleeding sores, and saturate her hungry soul, once and for all. The cry of the poet is not lost in the wilderness. I live through her verse, compelling her readers to reflect upon her loneliness, her craving, to love and be loved.

> ... I see you go away from me
> And feel the loss if love I never
> Once received. ("The Sea Shore").

Works Cited

Arora, K. Sudhir, "Voicing for Space", *Contemporary Indian women Poetry in English,* ed. Nibir K. Ghosh, Vol. 8, No. 1, a March 2009.

Das, Kamala, "An Introduction", *Indian English Poetry since 1950 onwards: An anthology,* ed. Vilas Sarang, Orient Longman, 1995.

— *My Story,* New Delhi, Sterling Publs. Pvt. Ltd., 1991.

Iyengar, K.R.S, *Indian Writing in English,* New Delhi, Sterling Publs., 1985.

Jung, Anees, "Outside The Frame", *Unveiling INDIA: A Woman's Journery,* New Delhi, Penguin Books, 1989.

King, Bruce, *Modern Indian Poetry in English,* Delhi, OUP, 1987.

Kohli, Devendra, *Kamala Das,* New Delhi, Arnold Heinumann Publs., 1975.

Milton, John, *Paradise Lost,* BK I, ed. F. T. Prince, New Delhi, OUP, 1972.

Nirmala, Mary, *Kamala Das, Only the Soul Knows How to Sing,* Kottayani, DC Books, 1996.

Pathak, R.S., "Indian Women Poets: Mapping Out New Terrains", 37, *Indian English Poetry: New Perspective,* New Delhi, Swarup & Sons, 2002.

Sarang, Vilas, Introduction. *Indian English Poetry since 1950 Onwards: An Anthology,* ed., Bombay, Orient Longman,1995.

Seemin, Hasan, *Poetry by Woman in Post Indipendence India.* Remarkings. Ed. Nibir K. Ghosh. Vol.7. No.2 Sept.2008.

Singh, Kanwar Dinesh. "Indian Women Poets in the New Millenium: The Post Feminist Phase", *Feminism and Postfeminism,* New Delhi, Swarup & Sons, 2004.

11

Revolting against Power Imbalance to Create an Unstained Future: A Feminist Reading of Kamala Das's Select Poems

—K.S. Anish Kumar

Writings of the present era deconstruct dominant discourses and open up new avenues of expressions. They concentrate more on the suppressed or marginalised, and present their oppressed condition by bringing out the cruelties that are exercised on them by the dominant setup. Most of the writers now insist the need to deconstruct the power-oriented system, which always suppresses the 'other' and pushes them to the periphery to maintain hierarchy.

Postmodern feminist writings focus mainly on the male-dominated society in which women are expected to live in silence, and are also expected to fulfil the needs of the dominators by satisfying their passions and daily domestic needs. The patriarchal setup started giving shape to its thoughts by creating its own versions of females through their creative writings. The so-called holistic and traditionally celebrated writings excluded the real aspirations of women. Contrary to this, women writers started writing their own experiences adopting male names in the beginning. In the beginning they were not only excluded from the dominant writings but also they were prevented from writings. After satisfying their roles as mother, wife and daughter they started writing secretly, presenting their problems through their females heroes. Their characters are not stereotypes but are "real women". They have started questioning the phallocentric system, which isolated them from time unknown. It is remarkable that most of the literary histories have excluded the participation and contribution of female writers. Hence they have begun to voice out their issues in their own language, which revolt against the vulgar descriptions and the stereotypic presentations of women.

Most of the women writers all over the world present the harsh reality before the readers by concentrating on the major issues like quest for space, identity and survival in the maleconfined space. They also politicise personal relationships through their writings and hence devalue the "holistic" concepts and go beyond the territories confined to them by the male-dominant institutions of power.

India is a country, which is known for its diversified culture and also for its hierarchical power structure. Many writers have presented the Indianess through their writings. Some celebrate India's unity in diversity ignoring the haunting reality. Kamala Das constantly presents the follies of the patriarchal setup and stresses the need to revolt against "the power-imbalance unequal society"

Kamala Das writes both in English and Malayalam. She started loving poetry (her favourite genre) at an early age due to the influence of her uncle, Nalapat Narayanan, a prolific writer and her mother Nalapat Balamani Amma. She has published poetry collections, namely, *Summer in Calcutta* (1965), *The Decendents* (1967) and *The Old Play House and Other Stories* (1973). When Kamala Das came to the field of writing her husband K.Madhav Das encouraged her aiming at the monetary benefits. In the early stage she waited until nightfall, after finishing her household activities, to write by using the kitchen table. Das recollects, "There was only the kitchen table where I would cut vegetables. After all the plates and things were cleared, I would sit there and start typing" (Warrior interview).

Kamala Das is a multifaceted personality who wrote poems, prose and sometimes she concentrated on painting and actively participated in politics. In all her fields she echoed the pathetic conditions of Indian women. She is of the view that in terms of culture and tradition women are imprisoned in the male-centred wall and to her the institution of marriage also exercises power on women. Her writings explicitly talk about sex without love and condemn the menfolk for creating such a scenario. She creates feminist consciousness through her writing. Her writings are compared with the well-established writers of the world, of like Atwood, Sylvia Plath and Anne Sexton.

Kamala Das's creative world universalises women's painful experiences through the authentic 'I' which often protests against the socalled powerful 'you', the representative of the males. She deals with the problems of women in India with powerful diction and with an extraordinary visual sensibility, which leads to photographic and cinematic effect. Her poetic world snaps the traditionally prohibited areas. Parthasarathy in his book *Ten Twentieth Century India Poets* rightly observes, "With a frankness and openness unusual in the Indian context Kamala Das expresses her need for love. What is over powering about poems is their sense of urgency. They literally boil over" (22).

Kamala Das's poems are the outcome of the intensely felt experiences and they try to explore the possibilities for an "unstained future". She articulates the need for change in the Indian mindset for it treats women as 'secondary'. She concentrates on the victimised position of women in the patriarchal setup and presents how the power of women is under estimated. "An Introduction" is such a poem written in autobiographical tone, which not only presents the quest for identity of an Indian poet but also focuses on a woman's quest for space in the phallocentred Indian set up.

> When
> I asked for love, not knowing what else to ask
> For, he drew a youth of sixteen in to the
> Bedroom and closed the door. He did not beat me
> But my sad woman-body felt beaten
> The weight of my breasts and womb crushed me.
>
> (*Commonwealth Poetry*, 48)

She visualises the cruel clutches of patriarchal setup, which uses the female body for its pleasure. The female body is violated and tortured, and the pain experienced by her is ignored or neglected. These lines remind of her first sexual experience narrated in *My Story* where she says, "Without any warning he fell on me, surprising me by the extreme brutality of attack." Escaping from the brutal attack is quite impossible in the rigid Indian setup. These lines also bring to light the cruelty that happens in the institution of marriage. It has become a place of power politics where the female victim is caught up in tight corners. S.D. Sharma in his article entitled "Kamala Das's Poetry", says:

> Kamala Das openly revolts against the traditionally accepted, strange, queer womanhood, concepts in the Indian society, which is so awkwardly full of abominable shams and cants. Rigid trammels of tyranny, she does not like at all. In a bitter piercing, cathartic tone, Kamala Das ridicules traditional imposters show of masculine strength and also man's lust (*Perspectives,* 3).

Repeatedly the traditional feminine role is imposed on women and their activities are keenly watched. Kamala Das says:

> I wore a shirt and my
> Brother's trousers, cut my hair short and ignored
> My womanliness. Dress in sarees, be girl,
> Be wife, they said, Be embroiderer Be cook
> Be a quarreler with servants
>
> (*Commonwealth Poetry,* 48)

Kamala Das clearly pictures how she is expected to adopt the role of a domestic woman but her intention is to break the circles which confines her in the male centered circle. As Iqbal Kaur remarks in her Prefatory note to the book *Perspectives on Kamala Das's* Poetry, her aim is "to reject the hollow prescriptions of society, to reject definitions given to women by men and encourage women to redefine themselves"(viii). Her move against the traditionally accepted norms threatens masculine power and her poetic mind is always in search of a harmonious relationship where love and security plays a predominant role. Contrary to this "his" mind is in search of a body, which can respond and satisfy his physical hunger. She says:

> You were pleased
> with my body's response, its weather, its unusual shallow
> convulsions *(Indian Poetry, 87)*

The pain involved in surrendering her own self including her physique and the resultant pain makes her feel completely deflowered and the loss of her identity for she says:

> You called me wife
> I was taught to break saccharine into you tea
>
> *(Indian Poetry, 87)*

She has lost her self-reliance and she is compelled to adopt a new role as "Wife" and hence hereafter she has to be always under his "monstrous ego". After becoming a wife she experiences the consequences of the exercise of power. She says, "I lost my will and reason to all your questions I mumbled incoherent replies." She has lost her will power for she is under the control of his artificial world—a world created by himself for him.

> Your room is
> Always lit by artificial lights, your windows always shut
> All pervasive is the male scent of your breath.
>
> *(Indian Poetry, 87)*

Most of the postmodern women writers, like Kamala Das, associate males with the world of artificiality and the females with the creative natural environment. Sometimes he is also associated with the inhuman natural world where he is reduced to a dangerous insect. To Atwood he (male) is a 'strange biological phenomenon' and to Kamala Das he is a 'old fat spider' also builds "webs of bewilderment". In that web she is imprisoned for his body is a prison, an embodiment of his monstrosity. His cruel appearance is vividly presented by her where his mouth is compared to a "dark Cavern" ("The Freaks") with uneven teeth. At the time of the sexual act, she says, the body responds without the willingness of the mind for the latter is in search of love. She explains:

> His right
> Hand on my knee, while our minds
> Are willed to race towards love.
> But they only wonder, tripping
> Idly over puddles of
> Desire ..... *(Indian Poetry, 88)*

The relationship that prevails between her and her partner is purely physical. She longs for love that comforts her. To her:

> Love means caring for another, having plenty of time for another. I want a kind of love that is pervasive – all pervasive like ether – love, which creates its own climate, a balming climate (*Perspectives*, 163)

Instead of creating a 'Balming climate' he is much interested in "skin communicated" relationship, which end in 'Vacant ecstasy'. She questions:

> Can this man with
> Nimble finger – tips unleash
> Nothing more alive than the
> Skin's lazy hungers?
> (*Indian Poetry, 88)*

According to Kamala Das he has failed to achieve love and is only capable of arousing lust, i.e., "Skin's lazy hungers". Her observations about her husband in her book *My Story* resembles with the poem. "I was in love with a husband who did not love (….) mine was a crushed love, a beautiful and futile emotion."

The passions, aspirations and expectations come to an end before the wounding sordid reality because the act of sexual love lacks mutual understanding and remains unfulfilled like the desire of the eunuchs in *The Dance of the Eunuchs.*

Unlike other women poets of India, Kamala Das presents man-woman relationship very powerfully and nakedly. Her powerful expressions sometimes threaten male-oriented set up and call for a revolutionary change. P.K.J. Kurup rightly observes: "Protesting the constraints of married life and male-domination she became a rebel. Her offended feminine self went on emotional wanderings attempting to explore an identity and freedom." (109)

Her dissatisfaction with the male confined universe makes her explore the possibilities of creating an anti-hierarchical society where equality and love play crucial role. To create such a setup women should understand their present victimised condition. She voices out her questions to her own folk.

Women, is this happiness, this lying buried
Beneath a man? It is time again to come alive
The world extends a lot beyond his sex feet frame

(*The Descendents*, 20)

These lines suggest that women should not under estimate their power and should not restrict themselves in the man-made vicious circles. Women should explore the meaning of life and move towards a place that provides security and comfort.

Kamala Das craves for a relationship which celebrates her presence and hence she dreams of an ideal lover, Lord Krishna. This ideal lover satisfies her expectations of achieving love beyond the physique. Her mystic association with Krishna can be viewed as a temporal escape from the real world, which injures her but the real world is more powerful and haunting where her lover's hands "travel beneath her dress and burns (my) her cities/down."

Kamala Das's poetry reiterates the idea that to create an unstained future a revolutionary change should happen in the existing setup which maintains hierarchical power structure. The need to change the hierarchical mind with the power of love is the under current of Kamala Das's poems. In her poetry as K.R. Srinivasa Iyengar remarks, "Love is crucified in sex and, sex defiles itself again and again" (677) and this is mainly because of the unequal status that prevails in the Indian society. In most of her poems her quest for love is more explicit and she tries to console herself with the mystic union with her ideal lover Krishna for human beings betray and limit her in their own perception like her husband for his body became my (her) prison and she says " I needed two strong arms around my shoulders and a soft voice in my ear. (qtd., in P.K. Kurup's "Contemporary", 111)

She stresses the need to change the power imbalance society, which victimise women and tortures them for their pleasure by treating them as "trained circus dogs". To change this endangered situation her poetic world articulates the idea that man should re–examine his hierarchical inner horizons and should come forward to create an altruistic anti–hierarchical setup which will pave way for an unstained future.

Works Cited

Das, Kamala. *My Story,* New Delhi, Sterling Publishers, 1996.

—*The Descendents,* Calcutta, Writers Workshop, 1967.

Iqbal Kaur (Ed.), *Perspectives on Kamala Das's Poetry,* New Delhi, Intellectual Publishing House, 1995.

Iyengar, Srinivasa K.R. *Indian Writing in English.* New Delhi: Sterling Publishers Pvt., Ltd., 2004. (Fourteenth Edition.)

Kurup, P.K.J., *Contemporary Indian Poetry in English,* (With Special Reference to Poetry of Nizzim Ezekiel, Kamala Das, A.K. Ramanujan and R. Parthasarathi) New Delhi: Atlantic Publishers & Distributors, 1996.

Narasimhaiah, C.D. (Ed.), *An Anthology of Common Wealth Poetry,* Chennai, Macmillan India Limited, 1998.

Peeradina, Saleen (Ed.), *Contemporary Indian Poetry in English: An Assessment and Selection,* Madras, Macmillan India Limited, 1987.

Warrior, Shobha, Interview. (http://www.rediff.com/news/1996/3107adas/htm)

Index